KU-578-668

Contents

About the authors   iv

Acknowledgements   v

One   Introduction: transformations   1

Two   Being a scholar-activist then and now   21

Three   Opening education and linking it to community   39

Four   Acting up, opening up knowledge   59

Five   Training scholars for the digital era   89

Six   Measuring scholarly impact   109

Seven   The future of being a scholar   131

References   141

Index   163

About the authors

Jessie Daniels is Professor of Sociology & Critical Social Psychology at Hunter College and the Graduate Center, CUNY. She has published five books, including *Cyber racism* (Rowman & Littlefield, 2009), along with dozens of articles. Jessie blogs at Racism Review and can be found on Twitter @JessieNYC.

Polly Thistlethwaite is Professor and Chief Librarian at the Graduate Center, CUNY, where she has worked since 2002. Prior to that she worked at Colorado State University, Hunter College, New York University, Yale, and the University of Illinois. Her activism with ACT UP New York during the early days of the AIDS epidemic primed her for present-day advocacy for public scholarship and open access publishing.

BEING A SCHOLAR IN THE DIGITAL ERA

Transforming scholarly practice for the public good

Jessie Daniels

Polly Thistlethwaite

First published in Great Britain in 2016 by

Policy Press
University of Bristol
1-9 Old Park Hill
Bristol BS2 8BB
UK
t: +44 (0)117 954 5940
e: pp-info@bristol.ac.uk
www.policypress.co.uk

North American office:
Policy Press
c/o The University of Chicago Press
1427 East 60th Street
Chicago, IL 60637, USA
t: +1 773 702 7700
f: +1 773-702-9756
e:sales@press.uchicago.edu
www.press.uchicago.edu

© Policy Press 2016

British Library Cataloguing in Publication Data
A catalogue record for this book is available from the British Library.

Library of Congress Cataloging-in-Publication Data
A catalog record for this book has been requested.

ISBN 978-1-4473-2926-8 paperback
ISBN 978-1-4473-2925-1 hardcover
ISBN 978-1-4473-2927-5 ePub
ISBN 978-1-4473-2928-2 Mobi

The right of Jessie Daniels and Polly Thistlethwaite to be identified as authors of this work has been asserted by them in accordance with the 1988 Copyright, Designs and Patents Act.

All rights reserved: no part of this publication may be reproduced, stored in a retrieval system, or transmitted in any form or by any means, electronic, mechanical, photocopying, recording, or otherwise without the prior permission of Policy Press.

The statements and opinions contained within this publication are solely those of the authors and not of The University of Bristol or Policy Press. The University of Bristol and Policy Press disclaim responsibility for any injury to persons or property resulting from any material published in this publication.

Policy Press works to counter discrimination on grounds of gender, race, disability, age and sexuality.

Cover design by Soapbox Design
Front cover: image kindly supplied by istock
Printed and bound in The United States of America

Acknowledgements

It may be unexceptional to note that a book is manifest by a collective effort, but the collaborations behind this work are extraordinary and plentiful.

We begin by thanking Victoria Pittman at Policy Press who suggested that the project should become a book. Then she offered invaluable direction and encouragement throughout the writing and editing process. She and many others at Policy Press, including Alison Shaw and Rebecca Tomlinson, were gracious and accommodating in their willingness to work with us to forge an innovative publishing contract that included significant author partnership in determining the format and distribution of this work. In a book that is very critical of academic publishing, Policy Press is one example of getting it right.

In part, this book is about the JustPublics@365 project, which emerged out of an initial conversation that included Juan Battle, Stephen Brier, Michael Fabricant, Michelle Fine, Ruth Wilson Gilmore, Janet Gornick, Deborah Tolman, and about twenty or so other faculty, brought together by Don Robotham under the Advanced Research Collaborative at the Graduate Center, City University of New York (CUNY). Don brought us all together to discuss how we might collaborate on interdisciplinary research on inequality, and in a flash of insight, he slammed his hand on the table for emphasis and declared: 'and, we have the *Internet* – we could use that to collaborate!'

Jessie Daniels took his declaration as a provocation and volunteered to write a short concept paper about what a project might look like that was collaborative, interdisciplinary, focused on equality, and using the Internet. From there, Michelle Fine and Deborah Tolman read and edited multiple drafts until they midwifed that document into something more like a fully formed grant proposal. Chase Robinson (then Provost of the Graduate Center) took an interest and invited Matthew K. Gold, an expert in digital humanities, to join the project. Gold, Robinson, and Daniels reworked the proposal over several weeks. And Robinson and William P. Kelly (then President of the Graduate Center) took the proposal to the funder. We are grateful to all of these wonderful colleagues for the shared experiences in developing the project on paper.

We were extraordinarily fortunate to have garnered the support of the Ford Foundation, which made it possible to take this experiment from conjecture to reality. We are especially grateful to Douglas E. Wood, our program officer at the Ford Foundation, for understanding the project early on, for guiding us through a time of tremendous change at that foundation, for stewarding financial support for the project, and for keeping the notion alive that social justice projects in higher education are not only possible, but crucial.

We launched JustPublics@365 with the help of a legion of wonderful colleagues and staff. Jen Jack Gieseking, Morgane Richardson, Wilneida Negrón, Brownyn Dobchuk-Land, and Colette Sosnowy offered their insights about the connections between digital technologies, scholarly communication and activism in ways that made the project so much better than we had originally imagined it. Emily Sherwood made every document that left our office look shiny and beautiful. Heidi Knoblauch led all our efforts at podcasting and managed MediaCamp. Stephanie M. Anderson and Amanda Matles created beautiful video recordings of our events. John Boy, Karen Gregory, and Fiona Lee offered creative and practical work on educational technology. All of these people did this challenging, often accelerated, work at the same time they were finishing their PhDs, launching their own careers and managing precarity. They are, each one, remarkable.

The JustPublics@365 project would likely not have happened at the Graduate Center if it were not for Matthew K. Gold. He guided the early stages of the project and helped maneuver it through the sometimes impenetrable institutional bureaucracy. His background in digital humanities informed much of the work we developed here, and we extend to him our deepest gratitude.

One of the key points we make in this book is that digital technologies open up new possibilities for collaborations between academics and journalists. This was a theory when we began, but our collaboration with the CUNY Graduate School of Journalism taught us more fully what is possible if academics and journalists work together. We want to thank our colleagues in journalism: Judith Watson, Amy Dunkin, Deb Stead, Susan Farkas, Frederick Kaufman, Amanda Hickman, and Jere Hester. We owe a special thanks to Sandeep Junnarkar, who did tremendous work to make the MediaCamp workshops a success. Tanya Domi, the Graduate Center's Director of

Media Relations, guided the op-ed workshop in MediaCamp's last iteration.

We are grateful to our CUNY librarian colleagues who worked generously and enthusiastically with us in exploring open access, scholarly publishing, digital preservation, research methods, and library-based activism: Jill Cirasella, Barbara Gray, Stephen Klein, Alycia Sellie, and Shawn(ta) Smith-Cruz. Shawn(ta) performed the bulk of the considerable legwork and author tutoring it took to open access to the #InQ13 course readings. Future reference to our work is possible because of Stephen Klein's indefatigable efforts to preserve the JustPublics@365 website and associated media, assisted by Suzanne Bernard. And, Anne Hays offered sharp and generous insight about how a publishing contract for this book might best be structured. We would like to thank colleagues at Hunter College, CUNY, where part of this work occurred. When we considered how to situate a participatory, open, online course in a specific New York City neighborhood, it was the material reality of a new CUNY campus in East Harlem that helped make that part of our project possible. The building is the result of a vision by Hunter College President Jennifer Raab, and a generous donation by the Silberman family, that strives to imagine a university doing well by the community that surrounds it. In a very small way, our project tried to realize this vision and it would simply not have been possible without that campus.

We are also grateful to community neighbors and partners in East Harlem who both welcomed us and challenged us to do better. Edwin Melendez, Director of Centro de Estudios Puertorriqueños (Center for Puerto Rican Studies) at Hunter College, generously opened the archives of their collection to the students in our participatory course and Centro was an essential partner. Marina Ortiz, of East Harlem Preservation, was an active participant in several aspects of the project and is an always thoughtful critic of newcomers to the neighborhood. Dr Marta Moreno Vega, Director of the Caribbean Cultural Center African Diaspora Institute (CCCADI), offered us a wonderful example of what could be possible in East Harlem and held our work to a high standard. Edith Velez, a community activist in East Harlem, offered her expertise on the future of public housing in New York. Ed Morales, director of the documentary film *Whose barrio?*, shared a rights-free version of his work with us. Arlene Davila shared part of her book, *Barrio dreams*, with us. Anaya-Cerda Aurora welcomed us to her bookstore in East Harlem, La Casa Azul, where we hosted several of our events. Iris Morales, (then) Director of the Manhattan Neighborhood Network El Barrio Firehouse Community Media Center, welcomed us into their studio for one of our events. Les LaRue, an East Harlem-based graphic designer, offered his beautiful artwork to make literal icons out of a dozen or so neighborhood heroes. We want to thank Caitlin Cahill and Wendy Luttrell, who agreed to the roller-coaster ride of being instructors for the #InQ13 course, an unconventional teaching experience, to be sure, that they both handled with grace and good cheer. Through it all, Edwin Mayora offered his expertise as a long-time student and researcher of inequality and resilience in East Harlem to help guide the project in the neighborhood.

We consider ourselves very lucky indeed to have so many friends and colleagues who willingly offer to read our work and provide feedback. Christopher W. Anderson, Cynthia Chris, Jill Cirasella, Kim Cunningham, Michelle Fine, Leith Mullings, Jules Netherland, Lisa Norberg, John Pell, Arlene Stein, Brett Stoudt, and Maria Elena Torre read various drafts of this book and their comments made it better, by bringing their perspectives from many disciplines and a shared commitment to opening the academy for the greater public good to bear on the manuscript.

Polly Thistlethwaite thanks Jessie Daniels for inviting this exhilarating and rewarding collaboration. And Polly lovingly thanks Liz Snyder for her abundant gifts of encouragement, entertainment, and inspration.

Jessie Daniels thanks Polly Thistlethwaite for being such a congenial co-conspirator in this adventure. As ever, Jessie thanks Jules Netherland for being her soft place to land.

ONE

Introduction: transformations

The Internet could seem like 'the invention of space travel,' writes journalist Ta-Nehisi Coates, who came of age alongside the rise of the popular Internet (Coates, 2015). For those of us who became scholars when card catalogs were the search engines of the day, the proliferation of digital technologies and the changes they have wrought can be at once exciting, puzzling and foreboding.

It can be exciting for those of us who became scholars because we love knowledge. The capacity to type any question into a small white rectangle on a screen and find millions of results can seem like the opening of new worlds, as Coates suggests. Being a scholar now means that almost all of us use digital technologies to do at least some of our work. We fully expect, even demand, that we will have continuous digital access to our academic libraries from anywhere in the world. We read, collect, analyze and write up our data within digital environments. Although some of us may remember when card catalogs, punch cards, and typewriters were the most convenient tools available, few of us would choose to return to those over our current scholarly practices. A generation of younger scholars has never known a world where 'cut and paste' meant to take scissors, cut paper with paragraphs typed on them, rearrange their order, and then glue them to another sheet of paper. For them, the Internet has always existed, and cut and paste has only ever meant the simple keyboard commands: *ctrl+x, ctrl+v*. Of course, this generation fully expects that their scholarly lives will incorporate these everyday technologies and an engagement with a broader world into their ways of knowing. Why wouldn't they? But, simply accepting this proposition makes it all too easy to minimize the profound transformation in scholarly life that is taking place. As with any change this weighty, it can also be, at turns, confusing and ominous.

1

'The only lasting truth is change,' science fiction writer Octavia Butler observed (Butler, 1993). While we may find comfort in nostalgic ideas of scholarly life as we knew it when we came of age as scholars, such nostalgia only obfuscates what's happening. The truth is that scholarly life is changing in multiple, and sometimes contradictory, ways.

Scholarly life transformed

The proliferation of digital media technologies is transforming a wide range of scholarly practices (Weller, 2011). If the *sine qua non* of being a scholar is creating knowledge, then this central endeavor is changing in all its component parts. How scholars acquire information to create knowledge, the mechanisms by which we find and read others' work in our field, the way we manage the citations of that work, where and when we evaluate the work of our peers, the ways we collaborate with each other, where and how (and sometimes what) we publish, how we engage in activism, how we measure success and how we teach are all changing. But these changes generate shifts in best practices for personal research methods as well as for policies and practices for academic review. For one, scholarship is opening, and with that openness comes new ways of working.

'I have been writing this book for the past four years, mainly through my blog,' explains Martin Weller (Weller, 2011). For Weller, the process of writing a book in 2009 was quite different from the process of writing a book just five years earlier. For him, the process was transformed through an array of digital tools. Weller details the list of technologies and resources he used for his research including: books – accessed via the library but increasingly as eBooks, and one audiobook; eJournals through databases at his institution's digital collection; Google Scholar; social bookmarking; more than 100 other people's blogs; YouTube, Wikipedia, Slideshare, Scribd; his Twitter network; Google alerts; and face-to-face conferences. Weller attributes the change in his scholarly practices in a relatively short timespan to the sheer quantity of tools: 'There is just more of this stuff around'. He also notes a 'shift in attitude (at least on my part), in the legitimacy of these other forms of output and their central, vital role in everyday scholarly activity' (Weller, 2011). Weller was certainly prescient in this regard, but he is by no means alone.

Scholarly publishing is changing. As recently as the early 1990s, when we (the authors) were both still in graduate school, scholarly publishing meant printed and bound volumes, distributed in hard copy to bricks-and-mortar library buildings for archiving. This is no longer the only, or even primary, way that scholarly publishing works. Across disciplines and fields, we now routinely compose work on computers, submit it to journals electronically, where editors send out papers for review through online content management systems like ScholarOne. Once the article is published, it appears in an online version of the journal, is indexed in an online database that tracks citations to that article and the journal as a whole. Beyond these mundane ways that scholarly publishing is changing, there are more profound shifts afoot that can be challenging to keep track of, let along make sense of.

The current model of academic publishing is suffering something of a legitimation crisis. Academic authors, like Kathleen Fitzpatrick, are critical of what many see as unsustainable contradictions in our current publishing systems, in which scholars give away their words and copyright in perpetuity to profit-gouging publishers. Much like Martin Weller did, Fitzpatrick began writing her book *Planned obsolescence* on her blog, where she pondered many of the issues she exposed in her book related to the potential of digital technology to reconnect humanities scholars with broader social debates, policy makers and general readers (Fitzpatrick, 2011). Fitzpatrick's practice with the blog-to-book also suggests some of the changes underway in peer review.

Before seeking out a publisher for the book, Fitzpatrick moved those early blog posts onto the Commentpress platform, opening it up to peer reviewers. The people who commented on her work-in-progress included high-level experts in her field, who she would typically expect to review her work, to graduate students at other institutions, as well as interested intellectuals and non-specialists from around the world. After a time in the open peer-review phase, Fitzpatrick published the book with a university press. Readers can still see the Commentpress site[1] and Fitzpatrick's earlier blog posts with her ideas in formation. For their part, New York University Press makes one chapter of the book available to everyone through its website.[2] Fitzpatrick predicts a radical change: 'I am certain that a revolution in scholarly publishing is unavoidable' (Fitzpatrick, 2011, p. 194).

There are multiple new models of academic publishing emerging. Today, scholars can use digital technologies to compile entire books that may (or may not) be subsequently published by well-regarded academic presses. This signals a paradigm shift to a world in which academic writing exists in abundance in many platforms, rather than in narrowly circulated bound volumes, whether books or journals. At this time, it is unclear which economic alliances will best support scholarly knowledge production in the future. What is clear is that models of scholarly publishing that view writing by academics as a scarce commodity – both difficult to publish and to distribute – no longer make sense in an era of comparatively cheap, digital production and distribution of scholarly work.

Reflecting on her experience, Fitzpatrick writes that these new platforms are changing the way we think about publication, reading and peer review: 'Distinction is no longer associated with publication, but instead with reception, with the response produced by a community of readers' (Fitzpatrick, 2011). She contends that digital technologies are broadening the definition of peer-review to include a wider range of specialists from inside the academy, as well as those from outside.

Being a scholar in the digital era means connection to the larger social world. In a recent survey of scholars using digital technologies, when asked what they saw as the benefits of using social media as an academic, many of those responding mentioned the connections or networks they had established with other academics and also those outside academia. Several made reference to the wide scope of these connections, which allowed them to interact with people across the globe and from diverse communities (Lupton, 2014).

The architecture of participation in the digital era has opened up new possibilities of being a scholar-activist. There is a long tradition of being a scholar-activist that embraces both academic rigor and using academic work in the service of the public good, such as W. E. B. DuBois who was both a world-class scholar and a leading activist (Morris, 2015). Being a scholar-activist is changing now, too. For instance, when researchers in Los Angeles observed that one of the top Google search results for 'day laborer' was a hate-filled site, they decided to take action. Researchers joined with community activists to create the *VozMob*, a project that utilizes mobile phone and web technology to address inequities that affect recent immigrants. *VozMob* involves community members who work as day laborers in documenting, analyzing, and discussing their own struggles by using a mobile phone to record stories that are automatically uploaded to the web. The narratives collected in the *VozMob* project help to counteract the flood of negative representations of immigrants, especially those who work as day laborers, in mainstream print, TV, radio, and online media (The VozMob Project, 2011). The reality is that when there are pressing social issues, digital media technologies enable scholars to connect their work to activism that is trying to address those issues. It is now possible for scholars to connect their politically committed work to the world beyond the academy in ways that aim to make a difference.

Being a scholar in a digitally networked classroom is changing, as well. Most mundanely, classroom management tasks like rosters, attendance, grades and course evaluations can now be done electronically. When grades are due and the university-wide grading system goes down, or the learning management system suddenly goes offline, the digitally networked classroom can seem like the iron cage of bureaucracy for the 21st century. When these are the primary, or exclusive, way that faculty (and students) engage with digital technologies, these can and do represent a menace. However, beyond managing the tasks of instructional bureaucracy, digital technologies can offer innovative routes to learning. Increasingly, college students enter the classroom expecting to learn in and through digital media. There are other changes to pedagogy that are shaping what it means to be a scholar in the digitally networked classroom.

The pedagogical style of the digital era is one in which the professor is the 'guide at the side' rather than the 'sage on the stage' (King, 1993). The diffusion of digital technologies means that students can, and often do, look things up on their own and it also means that instructors are learning about new developments in a field along with their students. In the last few years, the assemblage of technologies that make possible massive open online courses (MOOCs) have sparked a renewed interest in conversations about educational technology. Indeed, there has been no shortage of hyperbole about the 'revolution' that these promise. However, many critics have pointed out that the 'sage on the stage' kind of instruction that most of these courses offer isn't that different from 'revolution' promised by educational television (Picciano, 2014) or indeed, from traditional lecturing (Watters, 2015). There is a great deal of discussion circulating about what kind of difference digital technologies make to learning and how this should transform teaching (Davidson and Goldberg, 2010; Beetham and Sharpe, 2013). What is certain is that students, especially traditional-aged students (18–24 year olds), enter college already immersed in a near ubiquitous digital media environment and expect to encounter those technologies in their courses. Being a scholar in the classroom means guiding students to help them make critical sense of the digitally mediated environment in which we find ourselves.

How we measure scholarly impact is changing. When our scholarly research is shared on and through social media, it leaves a kind of data trail. The number of hits, downloads, shares, and other measures are easy to find on most social networking sites. There are many ways that these new metrics interact with more traditional measures of scholarly impact. For instance, there is evidence that when a scholar shares their research on social media, it is cited more often in the peer-reviewed literature (Eysenbach, 2011). There is a growing array of digital tools that combine the metrics shared on social media with those in traditional journals. The use of these new tools and metrics is uneven across academic institutions.

Our personal experience

The *terra firma* of scholarly practice is changing. From knowledge creation, publishing, collaborating and scholar-activism to teaching and measuring scholarly impact, digital technologies are changing the way we do our jobs as scholars. We will have even more to say about this later in the book, in particular about how digital technologies are opening up new types of collaborations with the goal of enlivening the public good. Whether these changes seem exhilarating, perplexing, sinister – or all of these at once – depends on a constellation of factors, such as position in, adjacent, or outside the academy, along with personal temperament and inclination to tinker with things. At the outset, we thought it important to say something about how digital technologies have affected each of us.

For both of us, digital media technologies are transforming the way we engage in scholarship and academic librarianship. I (Daniels) have chronicled the way a tweet at an academic conference became a blog post, then a series of blog posts, and then an article in a peer-reviewed journal (Daniels, 2013). For me, the use of digital media is transforming how I approach being a scholar. Twitter is not simply a tool for disseminating research; it's a tool I think with and through. Blogging is often the way I compose a first draft of a thought that I may develop further for publication elsewhere, which I have done in my scholarly blog, *Racism Review*.[3] For me, the blog is also a form of scholar-activism, a way to engage beyond the academy about one of the most pressing issues of our day. Though a generation (or two) older than those referred to as 'digital natives', I enjoy tinkering with technology. At an earlier point in my career, I left an academic post to work in the Internet industry. I came back into academia through a research project based at Rikers Island, New York City's largest jail, whose goal was to help young men returning to their home communities. This rather unconventional career trajectory has led me to consider the ways to join my scholarly work with both digital technologies and social justice.

As an academic librarian, I (Thistlethwaite) deal with the implications of digital media technologies on scholarly work every day. As students enter graduate school with digital skill sets and research interests, their more established, but less digitally fluent, advisors often struggle to understand how new media and tools work and whether what students construct with them bears any resemblance to what they understand as scholarship. The primary product of graduate work, the dissertation, is now a site of contested practice as small publishers, nervous about the threat to their business model posed by open access distribution, warn faculty advisors to caution graduate authors against current digital archiving and public distribution practices (Cirasella and Thistlethwaite, 2016). Such advice reflects an abundance of caution about a publisher's business model with less concern for the public good. In working with faculty, I increasingly serve as a guide on the complicated nuances of copyright and open access to scholarly work. As librarians, we constantly learn new ways of doing things.

The transformation of scholarly life that we have experienced is happening within a broader social and political context that is troubling for academic institutions.

Moving from legacy scholarship to digital scholarship

'When I was a student at Oxford,' scholar-librarian Robert Darnton explains, 'you had to slip between rows of fixed and revolving spikes,' in order to gain entry to the libraries walled inside the colleges (Darnton, 2012, p. 3). In this way, outsiders were kept at bay from the intellectual life inside Oxford through the imposing external architecture. The contemporary versions of spikes and walls are familiar to anyone who has been on a college campus recently, 'from locked doors and turnstiles to restrictive qualifications for entry, payment to obtain a reader's card and an atmosphere of intimidation.' Even beyond these obstacles, now, 'the most important barriers to knowledge are invisible' (Darnton, 2012, p. 4). For those without a university ID card, academic libraries can be forbidding places. The fortress-like quality of academic libraries serves as a useful metaphor for legacy scholarship.

Legacy scholarship is rooted in 20th-century (and earlier) analog practices of print publication, with little focus on conversing with others outside the scholarly world (Stein and Daniels, 2016). Legacy scholarship refers to a set of analog practices shared by academics working across disciplines. Under the legacy model, authors work in solitude to research and synthesize text for publication in printed, bound books or journals with small print runs made available to other scholars with privileged access to them through university libraries. This model produced knowledge exclusively for consumption by a small circle of academic specialists in the same or similar fields. The legacy model of publishing is concerned primarily with peer scholar-to-peer scholar review and is disengaged from readers unaffiliated with the academy.

Many of our methods of teaching are also rooted in legacy systems and 20th-century models of industrial production. According to Cathy N. Davidson and David Theo Goldberg, the practice of lining up and bolting student seats to the ground, in regimented columns and rows, with a teacher at the helm, was designed to instill the kind of work habits that conform to conditions of industrial capitalism. In the 21st century, we have a generation of students who have grown up with digital technologies, entering a very different kind of workforce. These students, they argue, require a very different kind of learning than the 20th-century version currently on offer (Davidson and Goldberg, 2010).

Digital scholarship, like legacy scholarship, refers to a set of practices rather than a single field of study. It is rooted in modes of knowledge production, distribution, and pedagogy that employ computer and Internet technologies. The digital age facilitates the development of different academic practices and new ways of engaging with publics beyond the walled-in academy (Stein and Daniels, 2016). Moving, remixing, sharing, and circulating information is easier and faster. Just as the *ctrl+x*, *ctrl+v* commands of cut and paste make it quicker to move text around than typing, scissoring, rearranging and pasting, other forms of digital activity allow for easier distribution and redistribution of text and all variety of media. The ideal of openness is intrinsic to digital scholarship. The rise of digital technologies has shaped the open access movement, which seeks to make scholarly books and journal articles available to everyone on platforms discoverable and accessible with an Internet connection. With the open access distribution and interactivity that our contemporary communications infrastructure makes possible, openness becomes not only possible, it is the default. The shift from legacy scholarship to digital scholarship is an important shift within academia, but is by no means the only one.

The contemporary academy is buffeted by two competing tendencies: commercialization and democratization (Darnton, 2012, p. 1). Darnton identified these competing tendencies in his scholarship on the history of books, and we contend that it also applies to the struggles within education writ large today. The forces that want to commercialize, or privatize, the academy are looking for ways to manage the 'cost disease' of higher education (Bowen, 2015; DeMillo, 2015), while those who want to democratize education want to make knowledge more available to more people (Suber, 2012; Giroux, 2014). Within these competing trends of commercialization and democratization, there is 'a dark side,' Darnton explains about libraries, and we would extend Darnton to include academia more broadly (Darnton, 2012, p. 2). 'Far from demonstrating uninterrupted democratization in access to knowledge, it sometimes illustrates the opposite: "Knock and it shall be closed"' (Darnton, 2012, p. 2). Darnton does not want to be construed as 'standing on some remote, moral high ground,' by making this argument (Darnton, 2012, p. 1). Instead, he wants to offer a more pragmatic path through down-to-earth contingencies toward finding a 'just equilibrium' between commercialization and democratization (Darnton, 2012, p. 14). We share Darnton's preference for the pragmatic, and we raise this discussion here because the widely held understanding of tendency toward commercialization in academia interferes with the trend we have set out to discuss here. We, as academics and scholar-activists, too often conflate the competing tendencies of commercialization and democratization with the transformation from legacy scholarship to digital forms of scholarly practice. This makes sense, to a certain extent. Scholars with a highly developed critique of neoliberalism[4] and an equally honed sense of social justice activism astutely observe the use of digital technologies for the purpose of new managerialism (THE, 2001). Given this critique, academics with an activist bent who want to resist commercialization may do so by steadfastly refusing the digital. "I will not be made to learn the Internet!" as a colleague of ours declaimed when he heard about our project. In our view, this is misplaced and reflects a misunderstanding of the forces at play here. What this misses, we contend, is the opportunity for digital technologies to open up new avenues of resistance to the forces of neoliberalism and corporatization of the academy. In our view, it is not only possible but it is imperative to be a digitally networked scholar who is also actively aligned with democratization and against the forces of corporatization.

Structure of habits for digital scholars

Digital technologies have radically altered the traditional structure of habits in the scholarly workflow. Digital sociologist Mark Carrigan describes the workflow of this way of doing scholarship as one of 'continuous publishing' rather than one with a clearly defined beginning, middle and end that the publication of a legacy project would involve (Carrigan, 2012).

In the appendix to his classic *The sociological imagination*, titled 'On intellectual craftsmanship', C. Wright Mills exhorts aspiring scholars to keep a journal and create a 'filing system' to reflect on personal experiences, notes about the literature in one's field, along with charts and diagrams. In this appendix, Mills refers to being a scholar as 'a choice of how to live,' he says, 'as well as a choice of career'. It is, he explains, about being a scholar, 'a structure of habits' (Mills, 1959). Mills was certainly a part of the legacy model of scholarship, and the practices he encourages are rooted there, but the advice that Mills offered remains sound, even though the 'structure of habits' is changing.

Writing practices are changing. Taking notes, a process that often starts or inspires research and analysis, can now involve digital practices and platforms. These more recent digital practices exist alongside analog practices. For example, when (then) graduate student Nathan Jurgenson got an iPad, he fashioned a portfolio case that held the digital device on the left side and a paper notepad on the right side. With this DIY case, he could take notes with a pen or pencil on the right side, and look up things on the Internet on the left side. His iPad case with a notebook illustrates the way note-taking both is, and is not, digital and analog at the same time (Jurgenson, 2012). More recent digital methods of note-taking sit alongside analog methods of pen and paper, sometimes in the same (modified) portfolio case.

Systems for organizing and archiving notes are changing. Word processing enables quick and easy editing, and linked metadata structures enable changes in one note to properly align with others. Now that academic journals are near fully online, article retrieval no longer requires one to locate printed copies on library shelves and then photocopy the desired pages. Scholars are developing a set of habits for using search engines, making decisions about what information is important and what is not (Löfgren, 2014; Lupton, 2014). Graduate students learning these processes look to faculty for guidance, but often rely on their peer practitioners and librarians to help them shape efficient digital research practices. One of the other basic habits of being a scholar, reading, is changing as well.

'Throughout the week I scan through the content that comes through to my RSS reader,' researcher Allan Johnson explains (Johnson, 2013). The problem of 'data smog' or the overload of information in one's field and allied interests can seem daunting, even unmanageable

(Shenk, 1997). Johnson uses Twitter to curate his reading and, in doing this, he has reimagined a crucial part of the workflow of being an academic: keeping up with the reading in one's field of expertise: 'The content is a mixture of my main interests: academia, of course, but also fashion, design, media, culture, theatre, and architecture'. He decides what to read immediately and what to read later based on how long it would take him to read a piece of writing. If he can read the post in less than 2 minutes, then he'll read it in the moment and share it (via social media) if he thinks it's worthwhile. 'But if it will take longer than 2 minutes, I send it straight to Pocket, a read-it-later app' (Johnson, 2013).

Reading is also changing, but in some unexpected ways. A recent survey in the US finds that reading in digital formats is increasing, with some 28% reporting that they read an eBook in 2013, up from 23% in 2012 (Zickuhr and Rainie, 2014). However, few have completely replaced print books for digital versions. In the same survey, only 4% of respondents said they were 'e-book only readers, while most people who read eBooks also read printed ones' (Zickuhr and Rainie, 2014). While we have not found a survey that specifically surveys the reading habits of scholars, our sense based on our own practices and talking with colleagues is that academics are following this general trend of reading a mix of digital and printed formats. As just one example, one researcher explained to us that his typical practice is to purchase the printed version of a book; then, when he needs to reference it again, he uses a digital version of the same book to search for key words and page numbers. Another scholar with failing eyesight explains that he has used text-to-audio converters, such as SpokenText, to convert written documents to MP3 files he can listen to without straining his eyes. Digital technologies are expanding the formats, styles and modes of reading, while printed texts in bound volumes endure.

The expansion of digital technologies means that our habits of accumulating and generating ideas are changing. Hundreds, even thousands, of digital tools like search engines, browser extensions, pdf annotators (for example Adobe Reader, PDF-Notes), databases (for example AcademicSearch, EBSCO, WorldCat), shared calendars, productivity applications (for example Evernote, ToDo), hot keys, code and document sharing platforms (for example GitHub, DropBox), are changing how we manage our scholarly work. Citation management, keeping track of all that work, is also changing. Platforms like Biblioscape, EndNote, Mendeley, RefWorks and Zotero offer new ways to organize and cite information. Some of these platforms go several steps beyond reference management, by enabling collaboration on gathering research, sharing notes and citations, and creating bibliographies; these citation manager platforms have the potential to change scholarly endeavor from a mostly solitary pursuit to one that is collaborative.

As in Mills' era, we are still likely to have a system of folders to organize our scholarly work, compile reflections, save charts and diagrams, and keep track of professional activities. Now, scholarly work is stored in folder-based paper filing systems that are invoked by icons, drawings on a computer interface we have come to refer to as desktops (Johnson, 1997). The difference in this shift from folders in a desk drawer to folder icons on a desktop is that the digital versions of this academic work can be easily shared with a network of scholars around the world and back again. To be sure, academics in a previous era shared work through postal mail, but it could be slow and, depending on where you lived, unreliable. The Internet speeds up this process and that makes a difference. Whether that is a feature (a good thing) or a bug (a bad thing) for scholarly life is a point of some debate (Carrigan, 2015).

Sharing academic work with colleagues separated by significant distance is part of what prompted the development of the technologies that became today's Internet. The fact that we can share our work across institutions and with those outside the academy is because of the successful and sustained investment in research and development in the information infrastructure of the Internet (Leiner et al, 2012). The earliest recorded description of the social interactions that could be enabled through digitally networked scholarship was a series of memos written by J. C. R. Licklider of MIT in August 1962 discussing his 'Galactic Network' concept, which he imagined as a globally interconnected set of computers through which everyone could quickly access data and programs from any location (Leiner et al, 2012). In practical terms, he envisioned the Internet we use today. Just as Licklider imagined, our 'Galactic Network' – or Internet – allows us to quickly access data and programs from any location. It also makes sharing work fundamentally easier.

However, the emergence of the popular Internet has not done much to change the sharing of work at academic conferences. 'Name badges are the central showpiece of a five-day game of scope and 'sneer,' says Rebecca Schuman (2015). While traditional academic conferences are one of the cornerstones of scholarly communication, they can also be intimidating, insular, and expensive affairs. Schuman references the Modern Language Association for her zinger about the 'scope and sneer' of academic conferences, but the MLA is by no means alone in the kind of status ritual she describes. Traditionally, such gatherings are only for other scholars, and are as closed off to the outside world as the academic libraries walled off and protected by the 'fixed and revolving spikes' that Robert Darnton described at Oxford (Darnton, 2012, p. 3). Further, what happens inside a conference meeting room rarely exists for anyone except those few who can afford to be physically present. While there have been some notable efforts to join activism with scholarly association meetings, these are often the exception that prove how unusual this is as a rule (Strauss, 2016).

Digital media technologies are changing the experience of some at academic conferences. As an alternative to the expense (and environmental impact) of travel to conferences, some scholars are creating virtual conferences through digital video and web conferencing or following conferences from afar via Twitter hashtags. But these are by no means replacing face-to-face academic conferences, which remain an enduring part of scholarly life. Digital technologies can open conferences to those unable or unwilling to travel. For example, backchannel Twitter communications can be an important mechanism for extending conversations with colleagues, organizing impromptu gatherings and forging new relationships. For those who use them, digital technologies can make academic conferences more open and inviting, both for those attending and for those unable to do so. Scholars who present at conferences can also share their work with the public, not just those attending the meetings, through open access repositories at their institutions or on commercial platforms like SlideShare.

Because so much of our writing and other work exists in digital format, it is far easier to share with others and distribute to large networks of other scholars. Today, academics routinely share work in digital formats as a matter of ordinary scholarly practice. Whether we do this by emailing rogue pdfs of journal articles smuggled out of our libraries to colleagues without access to the same databases, or legitimately post pre-print and pre-formatted versions of our work in an institutional repository or a commercial platform like Academia.edu, easy shareability is transforming what we do. Beyond this, some scholars employ a complexly layered set of digital technologies to collaborate. FemTechNet, for example, is a global network of feminist scholars and artists who work on technology, science, and feminism (FemTechNet, 2015). This group meets regularly online to further a wide range of projects, using video conferencing, cloud-based documents that can be shared and edited in real time, and a website that houses documents, archives videos, and hosts asynchronous discussion boards.

The ever-changing pastiche of digital technologies, alongside the analog of occasional in-person meetings, enables a new level of connectedness among scholars across geographic distance and types of institutions. Sharing research interests and exchanging work among scholars has never been easier. For many scholars, the broadening of networks makes connecting with activists a logical next step, but some have been doing this for decades.

Transformations in context

The rapid expansion of changes wrought by digital technologies can seem quite foreboding given the current landscape of higher education. Public funding of higher education is plummeting. Even though there has been growing student demand for higher education since the mid-1970s in the US, economic investment in higher education has been falling since about 1980. If current trends continue, some predict that state fiscal support for higher education will zero out by the year 2059 (Mortenson, 2012). This sharp decline in funding for higher education in the US is an attack on the very idea of the university as a public good through the market-driven policies rooted in neoliberalism (Giroux, 2014). An array of functions within the university – from food services to human resources – are being privatized, and even faculty positions are being whittled away. In the US, the number of available full-time, tenure-track positions is fewer and fewer each year, while those in precarious adjunct positions now provide the majority of college teaching. Most of the faculty on American college and university campuses are contingent employees (part-time in some form or fashion) (Street et al, 2012). A report by the American Association of University Professors (AAUP) charts the trend in faculty status over the decades since 1975, when 57% of all faculty positions were tenured or tenure-line,[5] and 43% were contingent. By 1993, those numbers had exactly reversed, with just 43% of all faculty in tenured or tenure-line positions, and 57% in adjunct or non-tenured positions. By 2011, the AAUP finds that only 30% of faculty hold tenured or tenurable positions, while the overwhelming majority, 70% of all faculty, are in contingent positions (AAUP, 2013). Some adjuncts, it's difficult to say what percentage, may have full-time jobs in their field and genuinely desire to teach only part-time. This scenario is more common in professional schools – law, business, medicine, and public health – but it is less common in humanities, arts and social sciences. The fact is that those who labor in non-tenured lines often shuttle between multiple campuses, must take on far too many courses in order to survive economically, and often work without benefits, including health insurance. The pay gap between tenured (and tenure-track) faculty and contingent faculty is widening (Lewin, 2013).

Stepping into the arena of the discussion surrounding higher education are a bevy of marketers, philanthropists, columnists, and writers without much experience but with lots of predictions about the changes wrought by digital technologies. Marketing guru Seth Godin argues that higher education is about to face an epic meltdown due to the rising cost of tuition and the wide availability of courses and information online (Godin, 2010). *New York Times* columnist Thomas Friedman claims that the 'MOOC revolution' will end world poverty (Friedman, 2013). In fact, as critic Audrey Watters points out, most of the promises and predictions for academia from such commentators have not borne fruit (Watters, 2015).

Politicians and university administrators increasingly demand business-style reporting from faculty about their teaching and scholarly productivity. In the context of austerity economics, college and university administrators must raise funds for their institutions to survive. Their jobs are tied to their fundraising, as deans at many institutions are evaluated on how much revenue they (and the faculty in their division) generate through fundraising. Administrators, in turn, pass along this pressure to full-time faculty, who must often raise part of their salary through grants. Institutions of higher education increasingly rely on business logics such as 'return on investment' and 'demonstrated economic need' to evaluate the worth of degree programs and research impact. In the UK, the funding regime of the Research Excellence Framework (REF) has institutionalized new measures of research impact with far-reaching, sometimes devastating, consequences for individual lives and careers. This expansion of an administrative class in higher education raises serious concerns about costs and neoliberal-style management practices.

"There's just a mind-boggling amount of money per student that's being spent on administration," says Andrew Gillen, a researcher who studies higher education. "It raises a question of priorities." According to a recent study by Gillen and colleagues, between 1987 and 2012, universities and colleges in the US collectively added 517,636 professional employees, which is an average of 87 academic administrators added every working day (quoted in Marcus, 2014). While there is debate about whether or not this rise in the administrative class is directly or indirectly driving the rising tuition costs, the fact is that this new layer of administrators is part of the larger political economy of higher education (Woodhouse, 2015).

The cuts in public funding, the trend toward privatizing services, the decline of full-time faculty and the rise of the 'precariat of adjunct labor' taken together have prompted cultural critic Henry Giroux to dub the time we are living through a 'neoliberal war on higher education' (Giroux, 2014). Take the growth of the administrative class in higher education, for example. It isn't simply a boondoggle (unnecessary, wasteful or fraudulent project) for would-be associate deans, but rather one more symptom of a larger shift in the economics of higher education. In addition to the thousands of regulations that govern the eligibility for, and distribution of, financial aid to students, the institutions themselves must generate income. Thus, there are entire administrative departments devoted to marketing to prospective students, recruiting and enrolling students (as tuition payers or loan qualifiers — on which the university takes a percentage), fundraising with private donors and chair endowers, grant writing, and managing physical space.

The buildings themselves, the physical space, are the focus of profit mining in higher education. The Educational Advisory Board, a consulting firm to higher education institutions in the US and Europe, identifies 'maximizing space utilization' as a 'top strategic priority at higher education institutions of all sizes', critical to 'stability of finances'. Increasingly, faculty are seen as standing in the way of the profit-centered goals around the physical space, for as the Educational Advisory Board describes it, 'faculty hoard facilities, refusing to give up or share space they do not need for fear they will not be able to get it back when needed' (Educational Advisory Board, 2010). It is common practice for institutions of higher education in the US to rent out the physical space of the university to paying customers from outside the university. Indeed, faculty and students who may believe they should be able to access their campus during off hours (when classes are not in session) may quickly realize that they are on a waiting list behind the paying customers who are using the space.

The rise in the administrative class of workers required to manage the physical space of the university is necessary if the goal is to implement the neoliberal vision of extracting profit from learning institutions at a time of decreased state support. The issue here for those who care about colleges and universities is not simply about the use of space or the cost of hiring people to administer these building efficiency schemes. The neoliberal logic that propels the need to maximize space, eliminate 'inefficiencies', and generate revenue becomes the script for how to run the university, including both the faculty and the students. In the neoliberal university that is low on public funding and heavy with administrators, the institutional logic is one driven first and foremost by the imperative to find and generate revenue. In the service of this goal, there is less faculty autonomy and shared governance as these get in the way of the efficiencies of the neoliberal capitalism. For teaching and learning, the neoliberal university places increasing focus on consistent curricula, delivered to as many students at a time as is possible, in order to move them all to degree completion as quickly as possible, so that they might enter the labor market as workers. Within this formulation, the university is no longer about fostering critique or engaging in a democracy as fully informed citizens. Rather, taken to its logical conclusion, the neoliberal university is a corporation, run by managers, with faculty are merely employees, processing the raw material of students (Savio, 1964).

Surveying the landscape of the neoliberal war on higher education, many observers mistake the rise of digital scholarship with the neoliberal impulse to commercialize the university. While it is tempting to dismiss the rise of digital scholarship as just another victory for the forces of neoliberalism, or, to get swept away by the rhetoric of the disruptive potential of digital technologies to transform all of higher education 'with just one click', both views are too facile. Understanding the complicated landscape of what it means to be a scholar now requires a more sophisticated appreciation of both the shift from legacy to digital scholarship, and the struggle between the forces of commercialization and democratization.

In academia, as elsewhere, we are faced with competing forces of commercialization versus democratization. The forces of commercialization, another name for the 'neoliberal war' that Giroux describes, compel higher education toward the 'maximizing of space utilization', the hiring of private security guards, cleaning and food services, and the 'adjunctification' of faculty, living at the margins of academe (Kraft, 2013). Simultaneously, the rise of the popular Internet has made open sharing of scholarship possible in ways that were inconceivable previously (Darnton, 2012). This broad conflict between forces of commercialization and of democratization is too easily conflated with the transformation from 'legacy' to 'digital' forms of scholarly practice. Not every form of digital technology is part of the long march to the neoliberal university.

This shift to digital scholarship is incomplete, uneven and entangled with the colliding forces of commercialization and democratization. Indeed, digital media technologies may be one of the best mechanisms for students and faculty who want to resist the forces of neoliberalism in the university and elsewhere. In our view, it is possible to both embrace the digital transformations in scholarship while also resisting the commercialization of academia. For many academics trained in the art of critique without the benefit of activism, it can seem inevitable that we concede defeat to the larger forces of neoliberalism and commercialization of the university and the demise of legacy scholarship. Instead of giving in to this nihilism, cultural critic Henry Giroux calls upon public intellectuals concerned about the future of democracy to speak out and defend the university as a site of critical learning and democratic promise (Giroux, 2014). The project we describe in this book, JustPublics@365, takes up Giroux's admonition and goes a step further. Our attempt at defending the university is also an effort to transform it.

Our experiment

JustPublics@365 was launched in January 2013 as an experiment in bringing together academics, activists and journalists, to address social justice issues through the use of digital media. It began in January 2013 at the Graduate Center, City University of New York (CUNY) (located at 365 Fifth Avenue in Manhattan). Several of us wondered if we might be able to collaborate in ways that fostered greater social justice by sharing it in the public sphere. This discussion took as its starting point the reality that we live in an era of rampant inequality. Media reports on inequality often gain little traction in a 24-hour news cycle dominated by the trivial. Activists work to address inequality in a myriad of ways, online and on the ground, but often lack connections to research or media that could further their causes and increase their ability to effect change. Key research produced by academics can help anyone grasp and combat the causes and consequences of the growing problem of inequality, yet this potentially impactful scholarship often remains disconnected from activism and locked within volumes and journals unread by the broader public.

JustPublics@365 was motivated by the notion that in order to fulfill its goal to obtain impact on the social movements of the 21st century, scholars must change their ways of distribution and communication with public audiences. Our experiment sought to leverage the reciprocal power of social activism and the connected platforms of digital media to meet demands for accessible and impactful information that retains the integrity and authority of scholarly research. We struggled, in various ways, with how to incorporate digital media technologies and social activism into an academic institution that is not necessarily designed to accommodate either of these. Despite our success at some of these attempts, we also failed again and again at what we attempted. In the chapters that follow, we will try to address both the successes and the failures of such a large, multi-faceted project.

Why write a book about a project that is steeped in digital knowledge production? Our goal here is to offer a vision about what is possible in scholarly practice if we take seriously both the capacity of digital technologies and the public good within the context of current debates about higher education. We do this in book format because we do not believe that books are dead. On the contrary, long-form writing in printed format will continue to be one element among many that bears scholarship into the future, enjoyed by academics, thinkers, and readers of all kinds. Books offer a particular permanence and transferability that born-digital formats still struggle to achieve. We thought there was value in bringing together the widely disparate elements of our experiment into one cohesive narrative that could anchor the project, and perhaps offer a guide for others in the *terra incognita* of what it means to be a scholar in the digital era.

While a good portion of the books written about higher education and digital technologies these days focus on how technologies may prove to be disruptive (or not) to the economic viability of colleges and universities, we take a different approach. Our focus is on the practices at the heart of being a scholar in the digital era. What follows in this book is a survey of the current landscape of higher education, a guide to what we've done, and a vision for what could be possible. For those who find these changes exciting, we offer a guide. For those who find these changes confusing, we hope to shine a light that makes a path forward a little clearer. For those who find the prospect of being a scholar in the digital era foreboding, we hope you find some solace here. Whether we embrace change or resist it, the ground beneath us in academia is shifting.

Structure of the book

This book is organized into chapters that can be read in the order we designed, or remixed in an order that suits the reader's interests. The order we put them in suggests our conceptualization of the project we describe, but you may want to skip ahead or back to read in a different order. In Chapter Two we look at the changing 'structure of habits' and explore how digital media technologies expand the possibilities — and necessities — of creating, collaborating, and connecting.

In Chapter Three we challenge the dominant MOOC paradigm and describe our attempt at doing something radically different and truly open.

In Chapter Four we take a look at the debates around open access and how digital technologies are changing the flow of knowledge outside and beyond the academy.

In Chapter Five we consider the unmet need of those who want to acquire digital media skills, and what it might look like to provide established and early career scholars with those skills.

In Chapter Six we explore the scholarship of engagement, trace the origins of the current system for assessing impact, examine the rise of 'altmetrics' and consider whether social justice metrics are possible.

In Chapter Seven we reflect on what the future holds when the digital is simply part of scholarly practice, and what is at stake in the battle over those practices within the political context of austerity.

Throughout, we begin each chapter with an overview of the current debates, move to a discussion of what we did in our project, and we end each chapter with a section called 'Forward thinking', to chart a vision for what might be possible if we truly reimagine being a scholar in the digital era with the public good in mind.

Notes

[1] MediaCommons Press, at http://mcpress.media-commons.org/plannedobsolescence

[2] NYU Press, at http://nyupress.org/books/9780814727881

[3] See www.racismreview.com

[4] Throughout the text, we use the term 'neoliberalism' to refer to a particular form of late stage capitalism associated with privatization, fiscal austerity, deregulation, and reductions in government investment in public goods and services, in particular, higher education. For more, see Brown (2015); and Giroux (2008).

[5] Tenure-line faculty are those who are employed full-time, typically with benefits like pensions and health insurance. Typically, after an extensive review period of six to seven years, tenure-line faculty are eligible for tenure, meaning that their positions are more or less permanent.

TWO

Being a scholar–activist then and now

B eing a scholar now is similar in many ways to being a scholar a century ago, especially for those interested in social justice. When W. E. B. DuBois and other activists in the Niagara Movement of the early 20th-century US wanted to spread their ideas about racial equality and social justice among sympathetic readers, DuBois bought a printing press. In 1905, he began writing, publishing, and distributing *Moon Illustrated Weekly*. Of course, W. E. B. DuBois was also a renowned scholar, a founder of the discipline of sociology, the first African American to earn a PhD at Harvard University (in 1895), and a prolific author of dozens of books that spanned the genres of non-fiction, fiction, and memoir (Morris, 2015). In 1910, DuBois held a faculty position at Atlanta University, but he resigned in order to begin working full-time for the activist organization, the NAACP (National Association for the Advancement of Colored People). There his primary responsibilities included writing, editing, and publishing the magazine *The Crisis*. The goal of *The Crisis*, like the earlier but short-lived *Moon Illustrated Weekly*, was to focus attention on lynching and other forms of systemic racism in the US. The analysis in *The Crisis* was intended to spur action to a more just and equitable world (Morris, 2015, p. 136). Guided by DuBois, *The Crisis* reached a wide audience, with monthly subscribers reaching 120,000 just a decade after it began in 1920 (Lewis, 2000, p. 384). In many ways, DuBois, with his prescient purchase of a printing press, foretold what it means to be a scholar in the 21st century. Being a scholar now, in the digital era, means that nearly everyone owns the means to create a document or a media file and a platform to distribute it through the Internet: a global distribution system.

Scholar-activism in the digital era

'A life of political engagement is so much more interesting than a life of private disengagement and consumption', observes Frances Fox Piven, a prominent social movements researcher. Pressing social problems prompt many scholars to join forces with activists. Piven says that by 'connecting with social movements, and developing your research in a way that is responsive to, and sensitive to, the aspirations and indignities that the social movements are preoccupied with', scholars can begin to address inequality. Developing research in a way that aligns with social movements is one way to do this, and one that Piven has experience with: 'I've done that. I don't think everybody has to do it, but I think it produces useful scholarship' (Piven, 2013).

When the Internet changed from one-way, read-only brochure sites to read-write sites where users could add, modify, and create their own content – referred to as Web 2.0, or the read-write web – it changed the architecture of participation, argues Tim O'Reilly. The read-write web is intrinsically designed for participation (O'Reilly, 2004). These changes in web technologies affect research practices as well.

Increasingly, the work of scholar-activists involves combining participatory research and documentary methods (Gubrium and Harper, 2013). For example, in 2013 a group of activists in and around Detroit, Michigan teamed with academic geographers on a project called *Uniting Detroiters: Coming Together from the Ground Up*, supported by the Antipode Foundation, to address problems facing Detroit and to develop collective analysis, reflection and co-research. They combined traditional research methodologies, like oral history and drawing maps that emphasized land justice, with digital activist strategies, such as documentary, that could be shared online and screened at local community centers to increase awareness and foster dialogue in the community. This group of Detroit scholars and activists also sought ways to use open data to further activists' goals. To accomplish this, they held a 'Data Discotech', with scholar-led sessions on using open data to support social change that was billed as a 'community science fair about open data' (Campbell et al, 2013). By combining traditional research methods with digital technologies, these Detroit-based scholar-activists were able to reach beyond the academy to engage people in issues of land and data use.

Another example of scholars combining traditional and digital methods for activist goals is *The Morris Justice Project* in the Bronx, part of the Public Science Project. Researchers Brett Stoudt and María Elena Torre developed the project to work with residents living in a heavily policed New York City neighborhood and created an active social media campaign in solidarity with court cases, legislation, and community organizing related to police reform. Since 2011, Stoudt and Torre have collaborated with residents of the Morris Avenue area of the South Bronx, a neighborhood in the 44th police precinct that then experienced New York City's highest rate of police stops that led to physical force. They joined together as a research team after each of them grew deeply concerned about the impact of the city's increasingly aggressive policing that targeted young black and Latino men. Their city-wide study confirmed a disturbing pattern in police harassment with youth (Stoudt et al, 2012, 2015; Stoudt and Torre, 2015; Torre et al, 2016).

Jackie, Fawn and Nadine, women living in the neighborhood, were already using their mobile phones to record police interactions with their children – mostly sons – in order to document the regular harassment they experienced. In a move that combined participatory research with digital media and street theater, the Morris Justice Project teamed up with the Occupy Wall Street artist collective called *The Illuminator*, who uses 'spectacular messaging' in the form of 'a Ford van with a light projector put to inventive and inspiring use' (The Illuminator, no date). As a crowd gathered, The Illuminator projected survey results onto a high-rise apartment building, while community researchers read the findings aloud over a mobile public address system (The Illuminator, 2012). Several traditional peer-reviewed research papers emerged from the Morris Justice Project (Stoudt and Torre, 2014; Fine, 2015). Like the scholar-activists in Detroit, those working with the Morris Justice Project combined traditional research methodologies with digital media technologies to promote social change.

Some critics argue that engaging in activism through digital media technologies promotes a shallow and passive form of political activism, disparagingly referred to as 'clicktivism' (Karpf, 2010). However, both the Morris Justice Project and Uniting Detroiters are deeply engaged with the political issues identified and embraced by a specific community, one in the Bronx and another in Detroit. These kinds of projects are only possible because of extensive collaborations. The paradigm shifts begun by emerging digital media technologies both enable and create a demand for different kinds of collaborations.

Convergence and collaboration

Scholarship, journalism, and documentary filmmaking have long had practitioners who straddled all these domains. Both W. E. B. DuBois and C. Wright Mills extended the reach of their scholarship by becoming journalists. Converging from another direction in the 1950s, American broadcast journalist Edward R. Murrow made social issue films that drew on scholarly research and helped shape the documentary's focus on injustice.

The proliferation of digital media technologies, and the increasing ease with which multimedia documentary can be produced, means that the products of scholars, journalists, and documentary filmmakers can become increasingly less distinct. Journalism schools frequently offer courses in digital media production; digital journalists possess the skills to craft news stories in multimedia formats. As these endeavors – scholarship, journalism, and documentary – become increasingly engaged with digital technologies, practitioners will collaborate and converge across the traditional disciplinary divisions.

Journalism

'I'm teach history and I'm often trying to convey to students its immediate relevance to the present – but in Ferguson I could see, very clearly, the way that the fraught relationship between the police and black communities has survived history and become part of the present', says Jelani Cobb (Queens Library, 2014). He traveled to Ferguson, Missouri after Michael Brown, a young African American man, was killed and after the grand jury decision not to indict Darren Wilson, the white police officer who killed Brown. Cobb, an associate professor of history at the University of Connecticut, also writes a regular column for *The New Yorker* magazine, where he reports on issues like the death of Michael Brown and the non-indictment of Darren Wilson. A scholar by training, Jelani Cobb has, like W. E. B. DuBois and C. Wright Mills, become a scholar-journalist to engage with social justice issues. He has also built a lively online presence and makes frequent appearances on network news shows, bringing his scholarly perspective as a historian to bear on conversation about the social issues of the day.

Transformations from legacy, print-only newspapers to born-digital online news are remaking journalism in ways that are both dreadful and promising for the public good (Anderson, 2013). The decline in print media subscriptions and advertising revenue has led to a dramatic loss of jobs in journalism, and it has especially hurt investigative newspapers and magazine research departments. Journalists, of course, are charged with doing the difficult, challenging work of holding elected officials accountable, offering sustained analysis in the public sphere and informing citizens about social issues.

'Citizen journalism' – everyday citizens using digital media to report news as it happens – holds promise for the future of the profession. Citizen journalists can work effectively together with mainstream journalists to make it more difficult for repressive regimes to control online information, but citizen journalism alone is unlikely to be the driving force in promoting social change (Xin, 2010; Khamis and Vaughn, 2012). Today, traditional schools of journalism are refashioning themselves to train would-be journalists in a new set of skills, including videography, podcasting, analyzing large, online, publicly available datasets – sometimes called 'big data' – and in data visualization tools, which allow huge, complex datasets to be rendered intelligible by a general audience. While citizen journalism will not save or replace professional journalism, citizens are augmenting the work of professional journalists.

Reading the Riots

When London police shot and killed Mark Duggan in August 2011, people took to the streets across England for three days. 'Politicians were quick to suggest a root cause – "gangs," said one, the "feral underclass" said another,' explains Tim Newburn, a social scientist at the London School of Economics (LSE). 'But, there was little public deliberation about it and no research' on which to base such opinions, much less public policy, which was worrisome to Newburn (2015).

When Louis Paul of *The Guardian* newspaper approached Newburn about an unusual partnership between researchers at the LSE and journalists at *The Guardian*, Newburn agreed (Devine et al, 2013). Together, they created *Reading the Riots* (*Reading the Riots*, 2012), a hybrid form of social science research and investigative journalism. In the short span of 16 weeks, a team of 30 academics and journalists completed 272 in-depth, face-to-face, qualitative interviews with 'rioters, with police officers, with lawyers, with victims, a huge number of others', Newburn says. The aim of Reading the Riots was to quickly produce evidence-based research that would help explain the events that unfolded in the UK in early August 2011. By early December of the same year, they published their results with *The Guardian*.

'What's unusual', Newburn observed in 2013, is that 'there isn't, still, a single, standard, traditional, academic publication from this study. Everything that's been published thus far has been published via the newspaper, either online or in the newspaper itself' (Newburn, 2015). Since then, Newburn has published several traditional academic papers on the topic, but the strategy to begin with *The Guardian* upends the conventional academic practice (Newburn, 2015).

As Newburn explains it, the traditional way that research projects like this one work is that scholars: 'dream up a project, hopefully raise the money, do the research, hope it's empirically sound, write it up, and then, right at the end, hope that you can get it out there in some way. So, now how am I going to get an audience for this thing?' (Newburn, 2015). The partnership with *The Guardian* gave Newburn the assurance that he would not need to worry about audience or whether the research, once completed, would be a news story. 'I never worried that it would be a story. It was *obviously* going to be a story, it was being run by a news organization' (Newburn, 2015; original emphasis). The reach provided by *The Guardian* news organization was huge, not just by academic standards, but by any measure.

'Our reach through radio, TV, a variety of other media, to opinion formers, politicians and the public generally, was massively enhanced through working with a news organization', Newburn explains about the partnership (Newburn, 2015). *The Guardian* estimates that they reached between 50 and 60 million people – staggering when compared to typical readership for traditional academic writing, usually in the low hundreds. 'In terms of media coverage, we had 30-odd pages in *The Guardian*, and in a variety of other print media across the world, not just in the UK', Newburn recounts, and '50 media interviews just on the launch day itself'. *Reading the Riots* also reached some in the highest levels of government in the UK, including the Home Secretary, the Leader of the Opposition, the Shadow Home Secretary, the Commissioner of the Metropolitan Police, and the Archbishop of Canterbury. Newburn and Paul presented evidence to the Home Affairs Select Committee, to the Victims and Communities Panel that had been set up by the British government, and won several awards in both higher education and journalism.

In assessing the project, Newburn sees advantages and challenges in the partnership. Along with the reach to an enormous audience, *The Guardian* provided access to world leaders and politicians, as well as to the less powerful. The challenges, he notes, are related to what he calls 'cultural differences' between academics and journalists. These have to do with the pace of work, flexibility and what he calls a 'can do' attitude among journalists that he identifies as missing among academics. He says that academics are behind the curve when it comes to producing other forms of media. In *Reading the Riots*, there are 'films, podcasts, a whole variety of other stuff, but nothing that looks like everyday, traditional social science … we're *way* behind news media organizations in the things that they can bring to bear in those fields. And we have a lot to learn' (Newburn, 2015; original emphasis).

The collaboration that made *Reading the Riots* possible was one that brought scholars and journalists together to look at a pressing, and current, social issue. Scholars are also beginning to work in close collaboration with documentary filmmakers.

Documentary filmmaking

Documentary filmmaker Dawn Porter sees many opportunities for collaborating with academics. 'If someone has written extensively about a topic, often you know the people that have really good stories. At the research stage, there's a great opportunity for collaboration', she says (Knoblauch, 2014). Documentaries are situated at the intersection of two important shifts: the lower barriers to the means of production and the changing distribution patterns. Today, there are simply more documentary films produced due to the rise in the independent and documentary film industry, driven by the lower production costs of digital video cameras and digital editing suites (Daniels, 2012).

Traditionally trained academics who are concerned with social issues see great potential in documentaries as a medium for raising awareness about difficult subjects with a wide audience (Daniels, 2012; Andrist et al, 2014). For instance, a landmark collaboration in the US between the National Institutes of Health, the Robert Wood Johnson Foundation, and HBO (a cable channel that primarily offers feature films for paying subscribers) produced *The Addiction Series* (2007), an award-winning collection of documentary films by some of the leading directors in the field (Bauder, 2007). The ascendancy of the documentary has led some critics to suggest that we are experiencing a 'golden age' of documentary, and it certainly is a heyday for scholars with the will and the desire to collaborate with filmmakers (Hynes, 2012).

Filmmakers rely on grants to fund their work, often from the same funders who underwrite more traditional academic work. This can stimulate collaboration. 'That's a really good collaboration, finding someone who will read over your submission to the NEH, or National Endowment for the Humanities. It's really critical', Porter explains. Filmmakers need to demonstrate to foundations and other funders that they are connected to the leading experts about the topic they are working on. This means that at the research and writing proposal stage in documentary filmmaking, 'there's a great opportunity to work together with academics who are interested in being storytellers', says Porter (Knoblauch, 2014). There are many other kinds of collaborations between scholars and filmmakers, as well.

Pink Ribbons, Inc.

'The idea of a documentary had not crossed my mind,' recalls Samantha King discussing the aftermath of her book, *Pink Ribbons, Inc.* (King, 2015). She just knew that she wanted to reach the widest audience possible with her critical take on the breast cancer industry. Then, filmmaker Ravida Din read the book. Din was drawn to the material because of her own experience with breast cancer and because of a long history as an activist.

Din called King, asked if she would sell the rights to the book and if she would like to act as a consultant on the film. 'I said yes right away', King recalls. She says that her main goal with the project – both the book and the documentary – is to 'engage a wider public in a critical conversation about the breast cancer industry'. The film made that possible in ways that her academic book couldn't. 'I'm sure that more people saw the film on the day it premiered in movie theatres than will ever read the book.' In addition to the theatrical release, King points to the reach of digital distribution, which has 'changed drastically from when the work first began'. Online video streaming services such as Netflix and iTunes have garnered whole new audiences for the work. The producer of the film, National Film Board of Canada, also makes it available online.

In all, it was a successful collaboration of scholarship and documentary filmmaking. 'I was so lucky to work with Ravida and the director, Lea Pool, both of whom I trusted implicitly', King reports. 'I didn't expect to be included in that way, but I'm grateful that I was' (King, 2015). Both the book and the film, *Pink Ribbons, Inc.*, are widely used by scholars, by community activists and in college classrooms. Yet, as much as the book and the film overlap, they also make distinct contributions.

'The book makes a contribution to the academic literature on breast cancer, women's health, neoliberalism, and social movements as well as perhaps to conversations in breast cancer and public health advocacy and activist circles' (King, 2015). On the other hand, the film presents many of the same themes but with greater visual and emotional richness. 'I think the filmmakers did a great job of emphasizing both the affective and political dimensions of the pink ribbon movement', says King (King, 2015).

Whether in large projects like the journalism–scholarship collaboration that became *Reading the Riots*, the documentary adaptations of a scholarly book into a documentary film, like *Pink Ribbons, Inc.*, or in smaller moves like an individual scholar writing for a popular news outlet, such as Jelani Cobb, or collaborating with a filmmaker on writing a grant, digital technologies are enabling journalists, scholars, and filmmakers to work together in new ways.

Our experiment: reimagining scholarly communication

'Probably my biggest angst about being an academic is that question of whether or not it makes a difference beyond just your students in the classroom', Melissa Harris-Perry said during a 2012 interview (Folkenflik, 2012). If we were to imagine a 21st-century counterpart to W. E. B. DuBois it might very well be Harris-Perry. She is a respected scholar, a professor of politics and international affairs at Wake Forest University in North Carolina, an activist, and the host of an eponymous weekend talk show on the MSNBC news network. Calling Harris-Perry 'the foremost public intellectual today', Ta-Nehisi Coates describes her show this way: '[it] brings a broad audience into a classroom without using dead academic language and tortured abstractions' (Coates, 2014). Harris-Perry's weekend morning show routinely featured two hours of scholars, activists, journalists, and documentary filmmakers from a diverse range of backgrounds discussing the social issues of the day. To increase distribution even further, after the broadcast the show was available as a podcast to download. Sadly, network executives failed to see the value in such an expertly curated and diverse program, and Harris-Perry's show was canceled in 2016 after a four-year run.

'One does wonder what would happen if the university would extend itself more productively into the marketplace of ideas', Ernest Boyer said in his famous remarks on the 'scholarship of engagement'

(Boyer, 1996). Boyer conjured a show very much like Harris-Perry's (20 years before that show aired), when he sought to reimagine the weekend news show of that day, *Washington Week in Review*:

> I find it fascinating, for example, that the provocative Public Broadcasting Service program *Washington Week in Review* invites us to consider current events from the perspective of four or five distinguished journalists who, during the rest of the week, tend to talk only to themselves. I've wondered occasionally what *Washington Week in Review* would sound like if a historian, an astronomer, an economist, an artist, a theologian, and perhaps a physician, for example, were asked to comment. (Boyer, 1996, p. 25)

What Boyer instinctively knew, and what Harris-Perry has demonstrated, is that there are productive, vibrant, and interesting conversations to be had across traditional lines of journalism or academia and that at least some segment of the public is interested in listening to these. Harris-Perry has extended this a step further, by regularly inviting grassroots activists on to her show for conversation with journalists, scholars of all kinds, artists, and filmmakers.

We drew on Boyer's idea of bringing together people with different kinds of training and background for a conversation on current social issues and on Harris-Perry's proof of this concept on her show. We wanted to try to create a series of events that were more like Harris-Perry's activist news show as a way of reimagining a key element of scholarly communication: the academic conference.

We also wanted to follow the model that the LSE and *The Guardian* created in *Reading the Riots*, with 'films, podcasts, a whole variety of other stuff, but nothing that looks like everyday, traditional social science', as Tim Newburn put it (Newburn, 2015). We wanted to reimagine academic gatherings in such a way that they could be open and could engage a world beyond those who could attend in person. We wanted to connect people across the silos that we were most interested in – scholars, journalists, and activists – around particular topics.

Along with this, we wanted to re-envision the conventional, and mostly closed, form of knowledge production typical of academic conferences. It is easy to realize in hindsight that this was an overly ambitious set of goals given our capacity, both in funding and in staffing. For the most part, our reach exceeded our grasp, as we attempted many things that turned out to be impossible. Nevertheless, we did produce an innovative series of summits, podcasts and eBooks around social justice issues, which may serve as useful guides for other experiments to come.

Summits

We hosted a series of summits in order to build connections among scholars, journalists, documentary filmmakers, and activists. Meeting in person, forming a connection in three dimensions and in real time, is crucial to journalism, to documentary filmmaking, to community-engaged activism, and to a good deal of scholarship. We called them 'summits' as a way to signal a shift away from the traditional academic conference of reading papers to an audience and to convey the sense that people would be meeting to create something together.

In early March 2013, we held a multi-day summit called *Reimagining scholarly communication for the 21st century*, to draw together people thinking through how research might be joined with activism through digital media. We invited the creators of an academic conference called *Theorizing the web* to host their conference at our institution as part of our summit, and several hundred scholars attended a lively day-and-a-half of presentations. To open that to a wider audience, we ensured that each session had a live video feed, and volunteers worked to send live updates via Twitter about what was being presented.

The other days of the summit included an #Occupy Data hackathon in the James Art Gallery, which features a large window opening onto Fifth Avenue, so that anyone passing by could observe the activity. The focus of the hackathon was to examine the socioeconomic patterns of first response to victims of the disaster that was Hurricane Sandy.

In the same gallery space on another evening, we hosted a conversation between artist Natalie Bookchin and scholar Alex Juhasz about their work together using YouTube to disrupt conventional representations of poverty. We also held several hands-on workshops, open to anyone, for those who wanted to get training in specific digital media skills during the summit and at the same location as the other events. We produced a panel discussion about 'altmetrics' – or new ways of measuring scholarly impact. We concluded with a plenary about what it means to be a scholar in the digital era.

In April 2013, we convened *Resisting criminalization through academic-media-activist partnerships*. This summit brought together leading activists, researchers, and journalists in small roundtable discussions about three crucial aspects of criminal justice: stop and frisk; the school-to-prison pipeline; and public health alternatives to criminalizing drug use. Telling compelling stories through visualizations is a key strategy for scholar-activists using a variety of media forms. An afternoon panel highlighted visualizing big data as a way for journalists, scholars, and activists to make complex data easier to understand by more people. Journalists, scholars, and activists presented interactive maps and large data sets displayed in compelling graphics. On that panel was Sabrina Jones, illustrator of *Race to Incarcerate*, a graphic novel (Jones and Mauer, 2013). Jones' innovative project is a creative example of reimagining scholarly communication. A gifted graphic artist, Jones takes Marc Mauer's landmark book of the same name on race, class and the criminal justice system, and renders a 'graphic retelling' of this scholarly book (Mauer and Sentencing Project, 1999). All summit participants received a copy of Jones' book. The evening plenary featured a screening of the documentary film by Eugene Jarecki, *The House I Live In* (Jarecki, 2013). Following the screening, we held a panel discussion with activists Glenn E. Martin (Fortune Society) and Gabriel Sayegh (Drug Policy Alliance), journalist Liliana Segura (*The Nation*), and scholar Alondra Nelson (Columbia University), the author of several works on race, health, and technology.

As with the first summit, we opened this up as much as we could to a wider public. All the panel discussions and the film screening were free and open to the public. We took out advertisements in local neighborhood newspapers in order to draw in more people from communities who are most affected by these criminal justice issues. Although the roundtable discussions were by invitation to scholars, activists, and journalists working on specific areas, we also had a video live stream and live tweeting from these discussions. Overall, we had more than one thousand attendees at the summits; among those were scholars, journalists, activists, and artists who connected across the usual silos of knowledge.

Based on our success with the first two summits, we were invited to partner with New York's Drug Policy Alliance (DPA) to extend the impact of their groundbreaking report *Blueprint for a public health and safety approach to drug policy* (Pugh et al, 2013). The DPA's *Blueprint* was the focus of a lead editorial by the *New York Times*, 'The next step in drug treatment' (*The New York Times*, 2013). In partnership with the DPA, we co-hosted a third summit at The Baldy Center for Law & Social Policy, University at Buffalo, State University of New York. Once again, we tried to open up this event as much as possible to a wider audience. This time, we did this by creating a podcast series based on interviews with scholars, activists, and policy makers in attendance. The podcast series was then made available on the DPA's website.

Social justice series of eBooks

For each of the summits, we created an online, social justice topic series that once again brought together activists, journalists, and academics. Rather than the face-to-face energy of the summit, the online topic series featured the work of scholars, activists, and journalists on our project blog. We asked people to write blog posts about the scholarship used in the key court case that had recently ruled that stop-and-frisk was discriminatory. We invited activists who had campaigned against stop-and-frisk to be interviewed for podcasts. We curated dynamic multimedia content from digital journalism, such as interactive maps that displayed the racial disparities of which groups of people were most likely to be stopped by the police. We interviewed filmmakers who screened their documentary at the summit, and we interviewed scholars and advocates who worked together to end the practice. Guest contributors were both people who attended the summit in person and also those who could not attend. One of our goals was to include contributors from each of the main sectors that we aimed to connect: scholars, activists, journalists, and documentary filmmakers.

These took different shapes depending on the focus of the summit. In connection with the first summit, about scholarly communication, we created a social media toolkit for academics (JustPublics@365, 2013b). While the summit highlighted the many ways that digital media technologies are making it easier for academics to connect their research with people, community groups, and movements that are also trying to bring about social change, many scholars we spoke to at the summit were still perplexed about how to use social media. We created the toolkit as a guide for scholars and as a way to deepen and extend the experience of the summit. We made the toolkit available in several digital formats (Pressbooks, Issuu and as a pdf), all freely available to anyone on the web.

All of this content appeared on our project's blog as individual posts during a specific and limited window of time, approximately one month before or after the summit. As each contribution came in, it was reviewed and edited by the project team. While the series was live, we shared each new contribution through the project's social media channels in order to keep public attention focused on the issue. At the close of the designated time period for the series, we compiled all of these posts into one eBook, freely available on the web in multiple formats (for example Issu, PressBooks, pdf, Kindle).

Imagining New York City after stop-and-frisk is the eBook that we created for the summit on resisting criminalization (JustPublics@365, 2013a). We created this eBook as a resource for use by activists, journalists, or scholars in the classroom. In it, we compiled a series of posts that had originally appeared on our project website, including: an interactive timeline of the practice; activist interviews and examples of digital storytelling about stop-and-frisk; and interviews with Jamilah King, a journalist who has been covering stop-and-frisk, and with Eli Silverman, a legal scholar and an expert witness in *Floyd et al vs City of New York 2013*, the case that ruled the practice unconstitutional. These different elements, written by project staff and outside contributors, appeared over a period of time, usually a month, on the project blog. Then, at the end of that designated time period, we would compile all the elements into an eBook and distribute that freely to anyone on the web who wanted to read it.

As part of this commitment to sharing knowledge beyond the academy and connecting it to activism, we also created a podcast series that took as its focus scholars working on issues of inequality.

Focus on scholarship about inequality: podcast series

One of the key ideas with the summits and with our project as a whole is opening up knowledge through digital media and connecting it to social justice. What might have been called 'knowledge products' in a previous era, we conceptualized as 'knowledge streams'. The idea was to bring people together both through the summits and through the collaborative, openly accessible eBook, and we did this. The larger goal was to reimagine knowledge production, which it did at least for the project team.

As many have pointed out, the idea of knowledge production is tied to 20th-century modes of industrial manufacturing (Davidson and Goldberg, 2010). As an advisor told one of us (Daniels) in graduate school, "If you were going to work at IBM, you would be expected to produce. It's no different going to work in a university, you have to produce something." In a previous era, when we were in graduate school, we were encouraged to think of scholars as creating 'knowledge products', bound journals and books with finite beginning and end points (the companion, and decidedly mixed, metaphor was about a 'pipeline' – 'always have a paper in the pipeline'). But for us, the knowledge that we were creating through podcasts, infographics, Twitter, blog posts, and interactive media or digital videos – all available to and intended for a broad audience beyond the traditional boundaries of the academy for use, reuse, comment, and remix – seemed more like 'knowledge streams' than finite products. Our ideas flowed outside of the walls of the university.

These knowledge streams are available to a broad audience and are designed to reach beyond the traditional boundaries of the academy to wider publics. For example, we produced a podcast series that featured interviews with scholars doing research on inequality and working toward social justice. Heidi Knoblauch interviewed more than a dozen people, including: Frances Fox Piven, talking about a lifetime of engaged scholar-activism around the rights of poor people; Juan Battle, discussing his large-scale study of over 5,000 LGBT people of color; Margaret Chin, talking about her research with immigrant garment workers in New York City; and Joseph Straus, explaining his work that connects disability studies and music theory (JustPublics@365, 2014b). The podcasts were available in a variety of formats, on our project website, through SoundCloud and iTunes. Over the length of the project, the podcasts were downloaded and listened to more than 540 times – not massive numbers, but a greater reach beyond the academy than most academic articles or scholarly monographs.

Changing the academy

The summits, podcasts, and social justice series of eBooks were successful in many ways. They offered an example of what might be possible if we were to open the academy and connect it to grassroots activism.

They were also failures in some ways. We underestimated the significant disconnect between the pace of 'Internet time' juxtaposed to the academic calendar and the slow pace of change within academic institutions. Within two months of the project start, we were fully staffed and hosting our first major summit. We were producing the summits, complex live events, while we were launching the #InQ13 course (see Chapters Three and Four) and the MediaCamp workshops (see Chapter Five). In many ways, our project ran at the pace of a digital media start-up within the context of a legacy academic institution. For many staff on the project, this pace caused problems, as it was too much at odds with the other aspects of their academic life. For other faculty colleagues, the pace and scope of the project was all just too much. As one colleague, Wendy Luttrell, described it, just one element of the project was *'dayenu'* – the word from a song that is part of Jewish Passover celebration, means roughly 'It would have been enough for us'. The fast pace and varied elements of the project at once were out of step with a traditional academic institution.

Planning and running events, such as the summits, that are creative and imaginatively conceived will often collide with the hard realities of academic buildings. Academic institutions, ours included, often have established protocols and structures that can be resistant to change and challenging to navigate. For example, when we wanted to host one of our events on a Saturday, we learned that the campus building was closed that day and it would require a special dispensation from the provost and an extra fee billed to our grant in order to open it on the weekend. When one of our partners for a summit wanted to help with catering by rolling in a cooler of beverages, we were told that all food and beverages had to go through the approved vendor for catering within the institution. Coolers of any kind were not allowed in the building past campus security. As another example, the auditorium where we held several events has a large sign affixed to the entry doors warning those entering to 'Please turn off your cell phones'. When we requested the sign be removed because we were trying to *encourage* people to use their phones to live Tweet the event, that request was met with the stony bureaucratic silence of unfilled work orders (the signs remain up).

The podcasts and the eBooks both met our goal of sharing knowledge beyond the academy and connecting scholars, activists, and journalists, but they, too, had shortcomings. While the Internet makes it possible to share information with anyone, distribution and sustainability of these new forms remains a challenge. We created eBooks and posted them on our project website, shared them through our social media channels and our networks, but people still had trouble finding them without the usual indexing of books done by libraries. The podcasts were hosted on accounts that required subscription fees to maintain. When funding for the project ended, so did the ability to host these audio files. Without an institutional commitment to the series or the content in it, there was no place for them to live within our institution's IT infrastructure.

The academy resists change. What we learned through our efforts to make change is that resistance is built into the very architecture of campus. We were also reminded that time and space are real, and that academic institutions operate at a different pace and rhythm than Internet start-ups. Yet, for those of us who want to know what might be possible, the summits, podcast series, and eBooks were a useful experiment in what could happen if we were to open up the academy and connect it to grassroots activism.

Forward thinking: creating, connecting, collaborating

From W. E. B. DuBois through to Melissa Harris-Perry, scholars in the 20th and 21st centuries have been interested in finding new ways to create knowledge, to connect to activists, and to collaborate with journalists and others beyond the academy. DuBois' prescient purchase of a printing press to launch *The Crisis* magazine and Harris-Perry's weekend cable news show of academics, activists, and journalists both speak to what it means to be a scholar-activist. Being a scholar now, in the digital era, means that nearly everyone owns the means to create a document or a media file and distribute it through the Internet: a global distribution system.

Scholarship that is intended for a small audience of other specialists within the academy and with no connection to the larger social world will continue to have a place in the academy, but there are indications that ivory tower-only scholarship is losing its appeal for many academics. Part of that shift away from cloistered knowledge production has to do with digital technologies. The architecture of participation in the digital era has opened up what it means to be a scholar. People are joining digital research tools with passionate political interests, mixing the methods of digital journalism with traditional methodologies of scholarly investigation. Being a scholar today relies in a fundamental way on the idea of open knowledge production, an idea that encompasses open software, open access journals, and open data. The ethos of openness is inherently tied to activism, in ways that might be unexpected.

Our summits, podcast series, and eBooks were experiments in opening up the creation of knowledge to a wider public. We also designed them to connect scholars, activists, journalists, and documentary filmmakers with each other to foster new collaborations and, ultimately, new knowledge once again.

THREE

Opening education and linking it to community

'We were on the front pages of newspapers and magazines, and at the same time I was realizing … we have a lousy product', revealed Sebastian Thrun, founder of Udacity (for-profit US educational organization), in 2013 (Chafkin, 2013). Just a year before that, Thrun had been leading the so-called 'MOOC revolution' with his venture capital-funded platform of massive open online courses (MOOCs), and predicting 'that in the future there will be 10 universities and Udacity will be one of them' (Tamburri, 2014).

In the fall of 2011, Stanford University – where Thrun taught – opened some of its computer science courses to the world through an online platform and found hundreds of thousands of students enrolling. The size of this response prompted Thrun to resign from his tenured position at Stanford and start Udacity as a company that would partner with colleges and universities to provide online courses, eventually replacing them as an education provider. Thrun's Udacity, and the millions he got in venture capital to launch it, quickly moved MOOCs from a niche discussion among educational technologists to the forefront of the conversation about transforming higher education (Clark, 2012).

The term 'MOOC' first emerged in 2008 (Cormier and Siemens, 2010) and four years later, the *New York Times* proclaimed 2012 'the year of the MOOC' (Pappano, 2012). There was no shortage of hyperbole about MOOCs that year, including *New York Times* columnist Thomas Friedman's suggestion that 'nothing has more potential to enable us to reimagine higher education than the massive open online course, or MOOC' (Friedman, 2013). So it was newsworthy when Thrun's Udacity, by then one of several start-ups in the MOOC-provider business, failed at San Jose State University.

Udacity's failed experiment in opening education

Thrun had promised that his work with San Jose State could 'change the life of Californians' by expanding access and lowering costs to college. Yet, after a semester in an online Udacity course, developed jointly with San Jose State faculty, students enrolled in the course did not fare as well as students who attended conventional classes with face-to-face instruction (Rivard, 2013). To explain Udacity's failed experiment at San Jose State University, Thrun said: 'These were students from difficult neighborhoods, without good access to computers, and with all kinds of challenges in their lives. It's a group for which this medium is not a good fit' (Chafkin, 2013). Although Thrun was quick to blame the students for the poor outcomes from Udacity's MOOC, there is ample research that finds no significant differences between online and face-to-face student achievement, and some conclude that online methods may lead to stronger learning outcomes (Koory, 2003; Bernard et al, 2004; Warren and Holloman, 2005; Fortune et al, 2006; Tallent-Runnels et al, 2006; Herman et al, 2007; Weber and Lennon, 2007; Dell et al, 2010; Means et al, 2010). This was also about the same time that Thrun was realizing 'we have a lousy product'.

MOOCs like the ones at Udacity are designed to work well for people who are already skilled at learning. One study of over 34,000 people enrolled in a Coursera MOOC found that 80% of them were people who already have college degrees; 44% had some graduate education (Christensen et al, 2013). This finding, and that the Udacity course failed to help students learn, comes as no surprise to those familiar with online instructional design. One of the key pedagogical variables that make an online course effective for students is time to interact with the instructor (Dell et al, 2010). MOOCs like the ones at Udacity, with video-delivered lectures to hundreds of thousands of students, and tests graded automatically by an army of teaching assistants, simply cannot enable one-on-one exchanges with the professor. Those interactions are the most important part of teaching and learning, and they simply do not scale.

The results of Udacity's endeavor at San Jose State should also come as no surprise to those familiar with education and inequality. Students who have gone to poorly funded elementary, middle and high schools get to college with an educational debt that has accumulated over time (Ladson-Billings, 2006). The fact that poor students may do less well in a MOOC that was not designed with them in mind is an extension of a systematic plunder of resources from their neighborhoods, schools, and countries of origin. Reflecting on what happened at San Jose State, Tressie McMillan Cottom, a sociologist who researches higher education, says, 'That's a consequence of an unequal, under-funded K-12 system.[1] You can't wall it off. Eventually you have to deal with it' (Cottom, 2013).

In light of Udacity's failure to 'transform the lives of Californians' at San Jose State University, Thrun announced that his company would pivot away from collaborating with universities and focus instead on corporate training 'working outside the world of college' (Chafkin, 2013). While many in academia cheered Thrun's departure from the world of colleges and universities, education writer Audrey Watters cautioned against unfettered glee. We should, Watters contends, be concerned that the bad pedagogy of MOOCs, characterized by 'short videos, multiple choice quizzes and robo-graders' is bad for all learners, not just those enrolled in colleges (Watters, 2013). Why should these pedagogical practices be acceptable for anyone, she wonders: 'Udacity's move may simply re-inscribe an education pipeline that filters out rather than opening access and supporting more people' (Watters, 2013). In other words, if those bad pedagogical practices become acceptable for some who already have educational advantages and all the other advantages that contribute to their place in corporate training rooms, this limits, rather than opens, access to learning. Opening access to learning is what the hype about MOOCs was originally all about – opening learning as widely as possible and connecting learners to one another.

Why openness matters

'Openness is critical to pre-Udacity rhetoric about MOOCs – it's striking how that's disappeared', said writer Aaron Bady at a forum about online education (Cottom, 2013). The original concept that drove the development of the first MOOC, created by Dave Cormier and George Siemens who coined the term, was a desire to open education, to foster community, and to build connections between learners that would continue after the course (Cormier and Siemens, 2010). The experiments in sharing the content of college courses that came before theirs, such as the OpenCourseWare (OCW) initiative at MIT, convinced Cormier and Siemens that content by itself was not enough to be transformative to higher education in any meaningful way. The true benefit of the academy is the interaction, the negotiation of knowledge, and the debate (Cormier and Siemens, 2010). Higher education at its best is an introduction to a life of the mind through contact with scholars who are engaged in the world of ideas. Being a scholar in the digital era brings the potential for more openness about what it means to be engaged in the world of ideas. One way of doing that is through opening our approach to education. There are many ways to open education, and digital technologies are facilitating this.

Increasingly, academics are sharing their strategies, resources, and struggles about teaching with others as they tweet and blog about their experiences in the classroom (Cormier and Siemens, 2010; Stommel, 2012). These digital practices are changing the structure of habits that surround teaching in a networked environment. In such environments, scholars move from discussions about their research to asking for resources to use in an upcoming class, much like academics have always done in conversations with colleagues down the hall at their own institution or at academic conferences. The difference that the digital makes is that it connects scholars at different institutions in geographically disparate locations, and amplifies those discussions in such a way that publics beyond the academic colleague down the hall can participate in them.

Opening education can also mean a different approach to curricula; moving away from standard class structures toward a participatory approach to curricula that encourages lifelong learning (Cormier and Siemens, 2010). There is a long tradition of participatory, learner-centered education that is intended to equip students with the skills and insights to challenge the power dynamics built into curricula, teacher–student interactions, and the educational, political, and social context in which they exist (Freire, 1970; Noguera, 2003; Davidson and Goldberg, 2010; Gardner, 2011). Opening curricula to a student-centered approach can happen without the benefit of digital technologies, but these can make it easier. For example, when performance and theatre scholar Kalle Westerling was teaching a public speaking class, he made the syllabus a collaborative document. The students in the class could comment on the syllabus and he could edit it. To begin each class session, he projected the shared document, and simultaneously, the students were also logged into the document. This made a difference in the class interaction. Students organized to propose changes to the syllabus. Westerling reports, 'It seemed that this made students pay attention to the syllabus in a different way than in any other class that I've ever taught' (Westerling, 2016).

Openness also means a shift in the role of the professor in the classroom. Rather than the 'sage on the stage' legacy model of a college classroom, a shift to a more open approach moves the instructor to a 'guide at the side' (King, 1993). As with opening curricula, this is certainly possible in a completely analog environment, but it is made much easier with digital technologies. When teaching within a digitally networked environment, being a 'guide at the side' makes more sense, as learners often have access to the same source materials (for example online databases of journal articles) as the professors. This shift is more crucial in a digitally networked environment, because it enables learning as participatory rather than transmission-based (Stewart, 2013). In a participatory course, whether entirely online, face-to-face or a hybrid of both, the professor guides students by filtering and curating information, while facilitating discussion and interaction (Cormier and Siemens, 2010, fig. 3.1). Through this more open educational process, being a scholar in the digital era includes more open approaches to teaching, curricula, and engagement with students.

It is in the opening of education that the transformative potential of MOOCs resides. 'If MOOCs are just free, open courses, then they're a public good', observes Aaron Bady (Cottom, 2013). However, most MOOCs restrict their course materials to paying customers – or at least, registered users. Even if users do not pay an upfront fee to enroll in a MOOC, the start-ups are harvesting registration data to monetize later. MOOCs like the ones Thrun created at Udacity are not 'open' by any meaningful definition of that word (Otte, 2012). Indeed, the typical MOOC is both enclosed and monetized (Straumshein, 2016).

The enclosure and commercialization of MOOCs

It is the much-hyped and well-financed MOOC platforms such as Udacity, Coursera, and edX that have received the most attention, and it is this model to which most people refer when they discuss MOOCs. The partnerships between Elsevier and edX (Elsevier, 2013) and between Coursera and Chegg, consolidating textbooks by Cengage Learning, Macmillan Higher Education, Oxford University Press, SAGE, and Wiley (Doyle, 2013), point to educational enclosure rather than openness (Watters, 2013). The MOOC models currently amount to a shaded variation on legacy models of scholarly publishing, in which colleges and universities pay for access to licensed academic content for a finite and regulated audience of readers.

Of widgets and blueberries: MOOCs and 'productivity' in higher education

Being a scholar in the digital age, or any other, means creating knowledge. Ask any scholar what 'being productive' means to them and they will likely think of the papers they delivered at conferences, or the articles and books they have published. But ask almost any administrator in higher education what the term 'productivity' means, and you may get a very different answer. William G. Bowen, former president of Princeton University and the Andrew Mellon Foundation, has much to say about productivity in his book *Higher education in the digital age* (Bowen, 2015). In defining the term, Bowen writes, 'productivity is the ratio of outputs to the inputs used to produce them'. Acknowledging that this definition is not very helpful, he continues:

> [B]ut this formulation conceals at least as much as it reveals, since it is maddeningly difficult in the field of education to measure both outputs and inputs – even within a single institution, never mind across institutions serving different missions. If only we produced standardized widgets or harvested blueberries! (Bowen, 2015, p. 2)

Bowen's lament here, which seems partly meant in jest, could be the howl of administrators in higher education everywhere. The dilemma of how to measure productivity, according to Bowen, is part of a larger problem he refers to as 'cost disease' (Bowen, 2015, p. 2). The basic idea behind this is relatively simple, writes Bowen: 'in labor-intensive industries such as the performing arts and education, there is less opportunity than in other sectors' – presumably making widgets or harvesting blueberries – 'to increase productivity by substituting capital for labor' (Bowen, 2015, p. 3). In other words, it is much harder to use capital investments to replace workers, as you might if your business was harvesting blueberries. As the hypothetical blueberry business owner, if your goal was to maximize profits rather than provide jobs, you could invest in a blueberry-harvesting machine to replace the human blueberry pickers. If only higher education were not a 'labor-intensive industry', then administrators could increase productivity.

For administrators like Bowen, productivity means outputs measured in the number of credentialed students[2] with degrees turned out by the university in the shortest possible time-to-degree, rather than in blueberries harvested or widgets produced. With this context of 'cost disease', Bowen goes on to discuss the 'prospects for using new technologies to address the productivity, cost and affordability issues' in higher education (Bowen, 2015, p. 43). This plainly states where digital technologies are situated for most administrators. MOOCs are viewed as a technological solution to the problems created by austerity politics that have systematically underfunded higher education over the last 30 years. Bowen, to his credit, sees the potential of MOOCs but remains circumspect about their ability to address these issues. He writes:

> It seems clear that MOOCs have an extraordinary capacity to improve access to educational materials from renowned instructors in various subjects for learners throughout the world. However, as far as I am aware, right now there is no compelling evidence as to how well MOOCs can produce learning outcomes for 18-to-22-year-olds of various backgrounds studying on mainline campuses. (Bowen, 2015, pp. 60–1)

But others are less reserved in their enthusiasm for MOOCs as a solution to what ails higher education.

In his book *Revolution in higher education*, Richard DeMillo unabashedly trumpets his enthusiasm for technology to make college affordable and accessible for a wide swath of the population (DeMillo, 2015). It is this kind of massively scaled teaching online, led by a 'small band of innovators', that will make the revolution of affordable and accessible higher education possible, according to DeMillo. In a section in his book called 'Is a university a business?', DeMillo seems to pose a question, but the only answer for him is 'yes, of course'. DeMillo has already answered his own question a few pages earlier under the subheading, 'Higher education is an Internet business'. For DeMillo, the problem of the current university structure is scale: 'one professor, teaching several large lectures, with the help of a small army of teaching assistants, can touch at most a thousand students at a time' (DeMillo, 2015, p. 123). This is not nearly productive enough, according to DeMillo. The problem he identifies is the same as Bowen: 'cost disease'. In other words, the labor-intensive aspect of education is a problem that the Internet's ability to scale up can solve. For DeMillo, the main problem with higher education today is 'cost' and the solution is 'increasing productivity' through massive scaling up of courses.

To scale up to massive levels, DeMillo predicts the 'rise of the super professor' (DeMillo, 2015, p. 123). Thus with 'five teams like this' – of a super professor and several armies (not just one army) of teaching assistants – 'we can teach five hundred thousand students' (DeMillo,

2015, p. 126). This is precisely the kind of change he has led at his own institution, Georgia Tech University, where he is the Director of the Center for 21st Century Universities. DeMillo partnered with AT&T and Udacity to create a computer science degree that is entirely online and offered at a lower cost to students, around $7,000, due to the corporate underwriting of the degree (Onink, 2013).[3] 'Exactly this kind of team approach was used in planning the Georgia Tech online master's degree. Two additional faculty members were needed to manage an increase of nearly nine thousand students' (DeMillo, 2015, p. 126).

In this view of the 'multiversity', the faculty are managers, processing students through the knowledge factory. The ratio of two faculty to nine thousand students is the sort of increased 'productivity' that administrators want to see realized in the academy through the use of digital technologies. But this runs counter to decades of research on the importance of engagement between students and professors (Picciano, 2002; Umbach and Wawrzynski, 2005; Wise et al, 2004). It also runs counter to the kind of pedagogy that teaches students to question and challenge the educational, political, and social context in which they find themselves (Freire, 1970; Noguera, 2003). For DeMillo, the only thing that is standing in the way of this revolution: faculty. 'The (MOOC) Revolution is an assault on the Ivory Tower – and its noblest ideas like scholarship, tenure + academic freedom that must be defended at all costs by holy warriors', writes DeMillo (2015, p. 223). The 'holy warriors' here are faculty, the ones defending scholarship, tenure, and academic freedom.

Leaving aside for now the important issues of tenure and academic freedom, given the focus of this volume, we want to consider for a moment what DeMillo has against scholarship. In his chapter on 'Brands' (Chapter 10), he writes a lot about football at colleges and universities, specifically the Sandusky sex abuse scandal at Penn State.[4] He uses this example to make the point that even though Sandusky's conviction on multiple accounts of sexually assaulting children in his care was damaging to Penn State's brand, the institution was able to recover because football is not the primary value of the Penn State brand. Its primary value is credentialing students. Scholarship is like football in DeMillo's conceptualization of higher education. DeMillo quotes Ben Nelson of the Minerva Project (a for-profit educational start-up), to explain it: 'If a student pays tuition, you can't say "Thanks for the money. I will now use it for something you don't want, like football or research." If you do that, your brand suffers and you eventually lose in the marketplace' (DeMillo, 2015, p. 221).

Faculty who insist on the importance of research and scholarship are damaging the brand of colleges and universities, by taking time, attention, and resources away from what should be their core, perhaps sole, function: teaching. Scholarship, like football, is a distraction from the main brand of teaching and credentialing, which are the keys to winning the marketplace, in DeMillo's view. The faculty, the 'holy warriors' according to DeMillo, are defending an old view of the university where scholarship, tenure, and academic freedom matter and digital technology does not. In opposition to these 'holy warriors' are the 'small band of innovators' – like Thrun and others – who are rethinking the university. In this view, the 'innovators' are aligned with the corporatist goals of credentialing as many students as quickly as possible. What DeMillo does not condone are the faculty (and students) who use digital technologies to engage in activism that challenges university administration.

DeMillo asserts that while digital technologies are all well and good as long as they are being used to secure a college or university's position in the marketplace, these same technologies are dangerous when used by faculty and students to resist the trend toward corporatization. In a chapter titled 'Governing in the age of Internet empires', DeMillo laments the use of digital technologies by 'mobs' of faculty and students. 'It is ironic that the same technologies the (MOOC) Revolution promotes can, in other circumstances, be turned on reformers and legitimate governing bodies', by which he means academic administrators and trustees. 'In the age of social networks, rules matter less ... and empower unaccountable mobs in ways that were unimaginable only a few years ago' (DeMillo, 2015, p. 247). To illustrate this, DeMillo offers several examples of 'unaccountable mobs' on different campuses that demanded (and won) the cancelation of a number of controversial speakers invited to give speeches at graduation ceremonies. To be clear, the 'small band of innovators' is using technology for good, while the 'unaccountable mobs' of faculty and students are using it for ill:

> Much as our small band of innovators uses online technology to remake higher education, creating vast communities of new learners and experimenting with new business models, mobs form easily in the era of the Internet, and a mob that grows without limits or accountability can just as easily become a governing force of its own. (DeMillo, 2015, p. 247)

DeMillo inadvertently makes a powerful case for why those in higher education concerned about commercialization need to be using digital technologies to mobilize against it. It is students and faculty – 'the mobs' – using digital technologies of the 'Internet empires' that have the potential to resist the agenda to privatize and monetize higher education.

The kind of MOOCs that DeMillo heralds as leading a revolution in higher education can be a commodity or a public good. As writer Aaron Bady puts it: 'Once market logic enters the equation – there is a depreciation of higher education. Then it becomes an ornamental luxury' (quoted in Cottom, 2013).

Our experiment: the #InQ13 POOC

With our project, we wanted to intervene in the discussion about MOOCs in a way that reaffirmed their potential for opening education and, simultaneously, in a way that resisted the imperative to monetize the experience. Our desire was shaped in part by our unique institution, the City University of New York (CUNY), which is awash with discussions about the promise and perils of open education made possible through an array of digital technologies.

The mission of CUNY is to 'educate the children of the whole people'. CUNY boasts a fairly recent past of free tuition for all students (CUNY Newswire, 2011). Given this mission and history, we were particularly intrigued by the potential for creating a truly open, online course that reflected that past, and reimagined what education for 'the whole people' might look like for the 21st century. With 24 institutions across the 5 boroughs of New York City and about 270,000 degree-credit students and 273,000 continuing and professional education students, it is the third largest university system in the US, and the nation's largest public urban university. The Graduate Center is CUNY's principal doctorate-granting institution, offering more than thirty doctoral degrees in the humanities, sciences, and social sciences with significant research on global and progressive policy issues.

A collective of approximately twenty people on our project created a participatory, open, online course, or 'POOC,' titled 'Reassessing Inequality and Re-Imagining the 21st-Century: East Harlem Focus'. The course hashtag, #InQ13 (for inequality, 2013) was adopted by the collective working to produce the course. The course was offered for credit as a graduate seminar through the Graduate Center, and it featured training in community-based participatory research methods.

Students who sought credit for the course enrolled in the usual way through the university. The course was open to the non-academic community for participation. About half of the in-person sessions were held at a CUNY campus in East Harlem and these were open to the community; anyone could watch videos of the course sessions online; and anyone could access the readings assigned for the course online. None of these modes of participation required registration, but those who registered and participated online experienced a greater level of engagement than those who did not enroll. In addition, we held a series of smaller meetings with community leaders about the course that increased awareness about the POOC and about CUNY's interest in East Harlem and potential for future collaboration.

A counter to the MOOC moment located in a community

We designed the course to engage with New York City. We were also concerned with providing a focus for the breadth of disciplinary approaches featured in the course. Several faculty who engaged in early discussions about the course suggested that we create an educational experiment that resisted the 'placelessness' of MOOCs by situating this course in a specific neighborhood. The MOOC moment in which our open, online course emerged influenced its structure and character.

East Harlem is a neighborhood that has simultaneously fostered a vibrant, multi-ethnic tradition of citizen activism and borne the brunt of urban policies that generate inequality. Several of the people in the #InQ13 collective had ties to East Harlem as residents, researchers, community activists, and workers, so the possibility of locating the course there was immediately tangible. In addition, Hunter College, CUNY, had recently opened a new campus supporting public health and social work in this neighborhood. These factors taken together – the unique, vibrant history and present of East Harlem; the connection to the neighborhood from those in the #InQ13 collective; and the new CUNY East Harlem campus – provided a compelling case for situating the course there.

So, the original questions that framed the course were joined by another set of questions: could a course such as this one 'open' the new CUNY campus to the East Harlem community in innovative ways? Given the troubled relationship of university campuses to urban neighborhoods, could we forge a healthy set of relationships? Were there ways that the digital technologies used in the course could offer a platform for community activists engaged in the struggle against the forces of inequality in East Harlem?

Community engagement with East Harlem began before the course started, and relationships took on more focused energy as course development began. Edwin Mayorga led these efforts as the official community liaison for the course, coordinating with 18 community partners (Daniels et al, 2014). There were also meetings outside of the course in East Harlem between the instructors, software developers, and community partners during the semester. Different parts of the CUNY Graduate Center also had to join forces in unprecedented ways. With POOC organizers aiming to afford every course participant unfettered access to course materials, a strong collaboration with librarians was required to create open access reading lists. The course offered lectures and discussions that were both streamed live and video-recorded, assigned readings, and set a series of assignments. Many of the guest lecturers were also authors of the assigned readings. This confluence provided a unique opportunity to begin discussions with faculty about sharing their work openly on digital platforms to global, non-academic audiences.

CUNY centrally licenses Blackboard software supporting password-protected course readings for enrolled CUNY students. (C)opyright@CUNY, a CUNY-wide library committee, posts guidelines and resources for CUNY instructors managing course reserve readings. Several CUNY libraries additionally offer SirsiDynixERes software and scanning services for local course support. Some CUNY Graduate Center faculty use Blackboard for reserve reading support; others use the CUNY Academic Commons and OpenCUNY platforms, both of which provide password protection for licensed course documents. Still other Graduate Center instructors employ commercial password-protected file-sharing sites (Dropbox and Google Drive, for example) to post course readings. A few instructors continue the analog practice of distributing photocopies, while others provide only assigned reading lists to students, who must find readings on their own.

The #InQ13 course could not apply these licensed course delivery platforms to serve students and lecturer-participants without CUNY affiliation. Similarly, our library-licensed academic works – journal articles, books, book chapters, and other media – could not be extended to audiences other than Graduate Center-affiliated students without violating license agreements. Assigning licensed readings for the #InQ13 course accessible only to those with Graduate Center credentials was antithetical to the goals of the course. Organizers refused to adopt a tiered access scenario that would only provide full access to course readings to some invited course participants. From the outset, there was little question that the readings assigned for the #InQ13 course had to be fully open access for anyone who wanted to read them.

At the time our course was offered, CUNY did not yet support open access publishing with an institutional repository, so CUNY librarians had to find a repository platform to support the course. Many of the #InQ13 authors unaffiliated with CUNY had posted works in their own university open access repositories. We directed several CUNY and non-CUNY authors to deposit works in the Internet Archive 'community texts' section that we established for use with #InQ13.

Structure of #InQ13

Each session was both live-streamed for those who wanted to participate synchronously and then, several days later, a more polished video recording of the class session was released and posted to the #InQ13 course website for those who wanted to participate asynchronously. The assignments for the course were designed by the faculty and by educational technologists (Daniels et al, 2014). Students posted their completed assignments on the course blog at the #InQ13 site. To facilitate group work, students could use a 'groups' feature on the site to collaborate around specific projects. As designed, these groups were intended to foster connection between online learners and CUNY-based learners, but the 'group' feature was not heavily used. The faculty provided feedback and grades on assignments produced by CUNY-based learners, and the digital fellow provided feedback for online learners (Daniels et al, 2014). At the end of the semester, students were invited to present their projects at a community event at La Casa Azul bookstore in East Harlem (this was in addition to the four regular sessions held in the neighborhood).

Libraries have traditionally offered faculty guidance about copyright by providing software and scanning services for reserved readings and by extending the use of licensed library content to a well-defined set of university-affiliated student users. Under current licensing models, this content cannot be extended any further, say to the massive, unaffiliated, undefined, and unregistered body of MOOC enrollees, without tempting lawsuits. As we see in the Georgia State University e-reserves case,[5] publishers will sue universities providing traditionally enrolled students with access to course reserve readings, even if the published readings are password-protected and selected according to reasonable interpretations of fair use guidelines (Smith, 2013). Though universities may open courses to anyone with an Internet connection and the will to participate, the vast majority of supporting course content, including academic books, book chapters, articles, and films, are not currently available to universities to redistribute openly. Course readings must either be published open access with copyright owner consent or licensed explicitly for open online course use (Fowler and Smith, 2013).

Kendrick and Gashurov discuss several potential models for MOOC enrollment and revenue generation that offer tiered access to licensed textbooks and scholarly material. Licensed textbooks and journals that are inaccessible to non-paying customers might be free or discounted for 'premium' paying MOOC customers, for example (Courtney, 2013; Kendrick and Gashurov, 2013). Coursera negotiated to license resources, just like libraries do, to expand access to textbooks and scholarly journals for their registered MOOC students. Access is supplied at a cost to the course provider, and it is limited to a pale fraction of scholarship available to university-affiliated students through traditional course reserve systems and, increasingly, through open access scholarship.[6] The Coursera and EdX licensing models ask universities to subsidize registered MOOC students' access to some licensed body of scholarly work, under defined terms, for some determined period of time. University-supported Coursera and EdX are poised to expand MOOC student access to academic content, but only within regulated, publisher-imposed limits.

The moment when licensed scholarly material is on the MOOC syllabus, the MOOC is no longer open in any meaningful sense. A course may be massive and it may be online, but its content is no longer open if students are required to register for access or encouraged to pay to gain enhanced access to course content. Restricted access is antithetical to the project of open access and eviscerates the transformative potential of MOOCs.

Jennifer Dorner says that MOOCs offer 'a real opportunity to educate faculty about the need for owning the rights to their content and making it accessible to other people' (Howard, 2013). Librarian–faculty collaboration in MOOC-building also involves conversation with authors about transforming scholarly communication. Activists, artists, and academic authors who participated in our course were invited to make their work openly available online through our course.

MOOCs offer authors a unique opportunity to widen readership and to raise the profile of their work. Prompted by authors' potential to increase exposure to additional readers through MOOCs, book publishers proved to be willing, and even eager, to make traditionally published works open access, at least temporarily and in part, if they were assigned readings for our open online course. Several book publishers, when approached by librarians, with an author being copied into the discussion, made copyright-restricted books and book chapters openly available online, particularly when the author appeared in our open online presentation series.

Evaluating the course, evaluating ourselves

The #InQ13 POOC was an alternative to MOOCs, emphasizing openness and participatory action above massiveness of scale. When the goal is for a course to be massive, the primary metric of evaluation is how many people register for the course. We took as our chief goal to create a course that was above all open and participatory, and this is much more challenging to evaluate. To do this, we considered a wide variety of measures to evaluate the course and ourselves.

According to what we could glean from quantitative measures, the #InQ13 course was a modest success. We had more than 8,700 visitors from 26 countries visit the course site. This is an extraordinary amount of interest in a graduate course on inequality, but it is modest when compared to the massive numbers that some online courses garner. We had a live video stream from 12 class sessions, and videographers created an equal number of more polished videos of these classes. These videos were viewed more than 2,800 times. Twenty students enrolled through the Graduate Center, and all completed the course successfully, as did one student who participated exclusively online. Several other students participated online but did not complete the course. Together, these students created over 240 blog posts and digital projects that they posted to the course site. The course hosted 26 guest speakers from the community and from different academic and philanthropic institutions. We held four classes as live events, open to the public, in East Harlem, and over 450 people attended these events, and another 300 or so participated in the course through the hashtag #InQ13. We also worked to make all the materials for this course, including the readings, truly open as a public good, rather than locking them behind a paywall. Altogether we offered 117 legitimately open access readings to readers anywhere through this course (see also Chapter Four).

Traditional measures of learning assessment are valuable, yet they often overlook the variety of learners and the wide range of their goals in engaging with such a course. Many people engaged with the course as lifelong learners, less interested in a certificate of completion than in an engaging dialogue about subjects that matter to them. 'I put it on and listen to it while I cook dinner, just like NPR', explained one woman via Twitter comparing the POOC videos to National Public Radio. A handful of online students revealed that they were interested in returning to graduate school, and so the course served as a way for them to experience a graduate course as a prospective student. A large portion of those who attended the public, in-person events were from the neighborhood of East Harlem.

The #InQ13 collective also included 18 community partners in East Harlem, and here we were less successful. The community partners we spoke with had several complaints about our project, all of them entirely valid. They said that we had come to them too late in the process, which we had. Our project, only funded for one calendar year, sometimes operated at a breakneck pace that was not conducive to the long, cautious process of relationship building necessary for community engagement. Several distrusted the university as a whole and, more specifically, objected to a course about East Harlem that was taught by CUNY faculty rather than by residents of the neighborhood. This highlighted the inequality between the university and the community we wanted to engage. If we had had the luxury of more time, we could have found more innovative ways to staff the course. Many residents who attended our live events at the East Harlem campus said that they were made to feel unwelcome in the building by campus security. This was not a particular complaint related to our project, but reflects a longstanding tension between neighborhood residents and the campus. As difficult as these critiques were to hear, we were grateful that so many individuals, groups and organizations in East Harlem were willing to support our endeavor.

Forward thinking: opening education for all

'A year from now we'll be talking about something different from MOOCs, but in my view, we'll still be asking essentially the same questions: How do we teach in digital networked environments?' predicted George Siemens, one of the co-founders of the original MOOC (Waters, 2013). This question remains for us the central one. Given the hype about MOOCs, and our experiment with the #InQ13 course, how then do we teach in digitally networked environments? Our answer to that question began with concrete interactions between a student community and a geographically specific city neighborhood, which called for a very different kind of model for learning, far removed from the broadcast teaching environments employed in most MOOCs.

While MOOCs have spurred discussions about online courses extending the reach of higher education institutions (and, in the process, proffering new, more profitable business models for them), our experiences with the #InQ13 course suggests that online courses that emphasize interaction between faculty, students, and broader communities are accompanied by significant institutional and economic costs. The #InQ13 course required at least 20 different individuals to produce it. Although college and university administrators envision MOOCs as a labor-saving, cost-cutting technology for higher education, our model offers an alternative. Our participatory, open, online course was, in fact, a job creation program. We employed more people, not fewer, through our version of a MOOC.

'There isn't one course format to rule them all', says Alex Havalais, former President of the Association of Internet Researchers and a professor at Arizona State University. 'MOOCs were and are just one potential collection of approaches to organizing a course' (Waters, 2013). The same year that we experimented with our POOC, several other variations on the MOOCs appeared, from 'small private online courses' (SPOCs) to 'synchronous massive online courses' (SMOCs).

The proliferation of these kinds of experiments by faculty and in ways that are not primarily driven by market considerations, suggest that there are profound shifts happening in the way that scholars in the digital era approach the classroom, the university, and wider publics (Losh, 2016). For example, Anne Balsamo, Dean of the School of Media Studies at The New School in New York City and Alexandra Juhasz, a professor of media studies at Pitzer College in Claremont, California, launched FemTechNet (FemTechNet, 2016) and what they called 'distributed open collaborative courses' (DOCCs), in which classes are organized around a feminist scholarship and the expertise is spread among the participants. Many of the instances of the DOCC were taught in community spaces, feminist bookstores, and one was held in a laundromat. The FemTechNet collaborative illustrates another way to think about communities – around shared interests and identity as feminists – rather than a geographically specific neighborhood. Both these experiments suggest a horizon of possibilities of opening up education in the digital era.

'This isn't just about MOOCs, this is about the democratization of learning', says Andrew Ho, an education researcher (Hazlett, 2014). Ho and research partner Isaac Chuang contend that institutions can learn something from these experiments. Institutions are beginning to appreciate how collaborations across institutions that involve many people beyond the traditional university can open up new routes to understanding. Those collaborations are 'making a difference around the world and back here on campus', Chuang says (Hazlett, 2014).

One way forward suggested by our experiment is to reimagine the digitally networked classroom connected to actual neighborhoods. It would be possible to create an ongoing course, like the one we did for one semester, as a more or less permanent feature of an institution. Such a course could be designed to be truly open, including all the readings, to anyone who wanted to participate, for an evening or for longer. Such a course might focus on a particular social justice issue that is relevant to that neighborhood, like water rights or land use or fresh food availability.

In this realignment of what such courses might do in a neighborhood, the primary function of the university becomes promoting civic culture, while the neighborhood promotes the advancement of learning. Ernest Boyer describes a similar engagement between a university and a city in Basel, Switzerland: 'The university was engaged in civic advancement, the city was engaged in intellectual advancement, and the two were joined' (Boyer, 1996, p. 25). To achieve this would require a substantial philanthropic investment as well as an institutional commitment to the course, but the return on that investment would be both a civic and an academic culture that is enriched.

Notes

[1] The term 'K–12' is a term used to describe the publicly-supported educational system prior to college in the US, and refers to the grades kindergarten (K) and the 1st through the 12th grade (1–12).

[2] Credentialed refers to anyone possessing a degree from a college or university.

[3] At the time of writing (January 2016), there are no news reports about how this degree program, or the partnership subsidizing it, is progressing. Udacity's site says 'check back' for progress updates. A question posted to Twitter by one of the authors (Daniels) about the status of the project got a reply from an executive at Udacity, which said simply: 'It's going great'. No other details were provided.

[4] In 2013, a total of 26 victims came forward to demand redress from Penn State College for sexual abuse committed by Jerry Sandusky while he was an assistant football coach at the college. Sandusky was convicted and is now serving a 30- to 60-year prison sentence for the abuse. In a settlement, Penn State agreed to pay $59.7 million in exchange for an

end to their claims against the university. For more, see www.nytimes. com/2013/10/29/sports/ncaafootball/penn-state-to-pay-59-7-million-to-26-sandusky-victims.html

5   The GSU e-reserves case is also known more formally as *Cambridge University Press vs Patton*. In 2016, a federal court found that Georgia State University's use of digitized course readings known as e-reserves is protected by fair use. The lawsuit, filed by three academic publishers (Oxford University Press, Cambridge University Press and Sage Publications, with support from the Copyright Clearance Center and the AAP), alleged that GSU administrators systematically encourage faculty to offer unlicensed digital copies to students as a no-cost alternative to traditionally licensed coursepacks, for which the publishers charge a fee. For more, see www. publishersweekly.com/pw/by-topic/digital/copyright/article/69830-gsu-prevails-again-in-key-copyright-case.html

6   See *The Dramatic Growth of Open Access Series* at http://poeticeconomics. blogspot.ca/2006/08/dramatic-growth-of-open-access-series.html

FOUR

Acting up, opening
up knowledge

In the 1980s, a new and frightening epidemic was devastating a generation of gay men. Remedies from elected officials and public agencies were appallingly slow or non-existent. Ronald Reagan, then US president, steadfastly refused to acknowledge the epidemic by publicly saying the word 'AIDS'. In response, a group of activists began to meet in New York City and formed the AIDS Coalition to Unleash Power, eventually better known as ACT UP. One of ACT UP's key strategies was to interrupt the business as usual – ACT UP swarmed public officials' offices and meetings, blocked traffic, and disrupted conferences, events, and even news broadcasts where people with AIDS were erroneously represented or underrepresented – in order to draw public attention to the HIV/AIDS crisis and to elicit action from policy makers. ACT UP members thoroughly investigated and explored HIV/AIDS and the conditions that sustained it, and became experts on the research and treatment of the disease. ACT UP brilliantly translated, publicized, and fittingly promoted, criticized, and supplemented HIV/AIDS research and reporting (or the lack thereof) by leveraging civil disobedience with skillful and persistent media outreach. Outraged that so many of my comrades, friends, and colleagues were dying, and eager to fight back against the neglect and hatred lashing back at queer people of all varieties because of this disease, I (Thistlethwaite) joined the group in 1988. Somewhat unexpectedly, it was through ACT UP that I learned to be an advocate for open access to scientific and scholarly information.

ACT UP members investigated medical and legal matters for political work and for friends. In preparation for every direct action, we held teach-ins and assembled fact sheets for activists in the group, for people who we encountered during the action, and for journalists. Activists prepared to talk to the press by learning about the issues, by incorporating our research into our visual agitprop, and by practicing delivery of a personally meaningful line or two. Members researched everything relevant to the crisis – from treatment options and drug regimens to economic inequality, mortality rates by zipcode, and legislative initiatives. We researched women's reproductive health, housing policy, policing strategies, racism in medical public health practices, sex work, and patterns of intravenous drug use. We explored how the National Institutes of Health (NIH) conducted clinical trials, then we critiqued them publicly and repeatedly, at one point staging a massive direct action protest at NIH headquarters. I spent many evenings and weekends working with ACT UP, and my day job also presented an opportunity for activism.

As a research librarian, I could invite guests without university affiliations into my workplace to allow them access to print journals, books, and research databases that were only available at that time, pre-Internet, inside library buildings. I was not alone in this work. There were doctors, nurses, lawyers, students, faculty and many other librarians who leveraged their credentials to tunnel into and 'liberate' the rich stores of information locked inside institutions of higher education so it could be used by non-academics who needed it. We connived and colluded for wider access to medical, legal, public health, social science, education, and humanities literature. All of it was valuable to further ACT UP's aims in some way. Yet, little of it was freely available to everybody who needed or wanted it, including the people who were dying from this disease. If I didn't fully comprehend it before I became a librarian, it was through this experience that I truly learned that access to scientific and scholarly information is a fundamental human right.

The emergence of digital technologies bears the possibility and the promise of openness. By the mid-1990s it was clear to us and many others that the World Wide Web could deliver electronic copies of books and articles, at low cost, to anyone with an Internet connection. In 2000, the British venture BioMed Central began publishing articles openly online. In the US, the NIH (alert to this issue because of ACT UP's constant barrage on the topic) and the National Library of Medicine launched PubMed Central, an open repository of biomedical and life sciences literature. PubMed Central was followed by the 2003 launch of the Public Library of Science (PLOS) and shortly thereafter by PLOS Biology and PLOS Medicine – all high-quality journals openly and immediately available upon publication to anyone. Digital technologies and the resulting lower barriers to publishing drove these developments, in part. These changes in scholarly publishing were certainly responses to activism that demanded free and open health and medical research.

For a variety of reasons, not least of which are different funding mechanisms, scholarly publishing in the humanities and social sciences has been less transformed by the digital turn. These fields predominantly still operate under legacy models of scholarly publishing.

The legacy model of scholarly publishing is broken

The legacy formats of scholarship – printed and bound volumes, circulating through closed collections, intended for small audiences of specialists – continue to shape scholarly production practices, but this does not work as well as it could for faculty authors, readers, and libraries

Academic authors

The way scholarly publishing works is difficult to explain to anyone outside the system, because it makes so little sense. Unlike literary authors, journalists, filmmakers or any other cultural workers, academics do not get paid directly for published work. We are paid as faculty members for teaching, for administration, and for research, writing, and even – if you include it in our institutional salaries – for publishing. When it comes to writing and publishing, academic authors operate in a 'gift exchange' culture, where we 'donate' our work and copyright to academic publishers for free (Borgman, 2007). While some academic book publishers offer small payments (in advances or royalties), most do not.

When publishing in academic journals, faculty are never compensated. Instead, they perform unpaid, and often invisible, labor in the form of peer review of others' work for journals. Work such as serving on journal editorial boards, and even editing journals, is also unpaid, but it does show up on a faculty member's academic résumé (or curriculum vitae), because it is an element of service required to be successful for academic promotion and tenure. In exchange, faculty receive the publishers' copyediting, formatting, and distribution of a work, and they gain the credential of a peer-reviewed publication that is required for their promotion and tenure. This line of academic credibility gets translated back into currency that academic institutions recognize and reward.

Financial compensation is one thing, and copyright is another. Again, unlike many other cultural workers, academics do not usually hold the copyright to their own work. Instead, under pressure of time to achieve and to advance, academics are encouraged to 'donate' their copyright to publishing houses. Those terms of donation are not usually favorable for the donating scholar. The standard copyright agreement that most academic authors sign gives away every right to publishers. Publishers retain authors' copyright in perpetuity – meaning until the author's death and beyond – unless authors make special, non-traditional contractual arrangements. Few academics know how or why, or can afford the extra time and effort to bother with this. Thus, for academic authors this publishing model offers a reliable form of credentialing, but it trades on 'donated' labor, enriches commercial publishers, and leaves authors without the right to freely distribute their own work, ever.

Readers

Of course, authors are also readers. The legacy model of publishing does not serve those who seek to read widely either. For example, Sarah Kendzior, a researcher for *Al Jazeera English* who often writes about publishing in academia, says:

> I have a PhD, I do scholarly research, but I am not affiliated with a university. When I am doing research, I have to use other people's logins/passwords in order to access the latest academic articles in my field – articles which often cite my own work. (quoted in Tadween Editors, 2013)

The legacy model of publishing assumes a small readership of academics who enjoy affiliation with a research library. To the users affiliated with a subscribing library, this privileged access is often invisible. Like shopping software that remembers a credit card number, library software has by and large succeeded in reducing repeated credentialing hoops that users must jump through to reach research articles and eBooks, facilitating a relatively seamless flow of credentialed access through personal devices once the login is initially applied. This can lull scholars with institutionally credentialed access to databases of academic journal articles into a false sense of universality, by masking just how rarefied that access is, at the same time that it makes access to scholarly literature more convenient for credentialed scholars.

People without a university affiliation encounter sharply limited access to academic research. Unaffiliated researchers like Kendzior or academics working outside wealthy universities in the global north – participants in or subjects of academic studies, non-academic partners in research, non-traditional online students, journalists, policy makers, public administrators, artists, high school and elementary teachers, and non-academic professionals of all variety – are locked out of scholarly databases. Often the information in those databases could bring some benefit to those who are locked out. 'Some people argue that scholarly work has limited appeal, but this is an elitist position', says Sarah Kendzior. 'You never know who will benefit from your work. The only way to find out is to make it accessible' (Tadween Editors, 2013).

One group that may know very well the benefit of reading in scholarly databases is college alumni. Most faculty would be delighted to learn that their students wanted to keep reading in the scholarly literature after they graduate, but that's not likely. Once students graduate and leave academia, they no longer have access to the literature they were exposed to and learned to read in college. Students who have paid thousands of dollars in tuition fees over several years and finally graduate are often shocked to realize that they no longer have access to library databases and other materials. Typically, if alumni have library privileges at all, they are offered access to a limited set of library-sponsored literature in their academic fields. More likely, alumni are barred, like most others who must either pay to download academic articles or come up with some work-around to get past restricted access to an academic library. Although state and city public libraries offer some limited sets of popular press and scholarly journals to card-holding users, those journal packages provide significantly fewer resources than a typical academic library does. The legacy model of publishing does not, in this very real way, encourage lifelong learning.

Profits

Five academic publishers – Elsevier, Springer, Wiley, Taylor & Francis, Sage – account for the majority of all the scholarly articles published globally, including some 70% of social sciences articles (Larivière et al, 2015). That's a dramatic increase from the 1970s, when those five publishers accounted for only about 10% of all scholarly articles. Since that time, mergers and acquisitions have led to an oligopoly of academic publishing.

Profit margins for these commercial publishers have grown steadily since the early 1990s. In 2011, the journal publishing divisions of Elsevier, Springer, and Wiley reported profits equal to 36%, 33.9%, and 42% respectively (Bergstrom et al, 2014). Astute observers at *Cultural Anthropology* note that academic publishers' profits were higher than those in several other industries in 2014, including oil (Exxon Mobil has a net profit margin of 7.31%), diamonds and minerals (Rio Tinto's profit margin is 13.69%), and even banking (JP Morgan Chase claims profits of only 24.57%). They conclude wryly: 'Volunteered academic labor, it turns out, is a far more lucrative platform for profit accumulation than fossil fuels, mineral resources, and international finance' (Jiménez et al, 2015).

Increasingly, these rising profits are driven by a pricing strategy called 'the big deal'. Like cable television providers who bundle premium channels with less popular channels to increase sales and profits, publishers and their distributors sell packaged journal subscriptions to libraries. The 'big deals' mean that college and university libraries spend more than they want on huge packages of journal titles that include duplicates of what they already license from other vendors, and more minor titles representing more fields than they usually need from any vendor, in order to acquire the mainstay journals they need to support their students and faculty.

Some legal scholars argue that these practices may violate international antitrust laws (Edlin and Rubinfeld, 2004). This raises an interesting point. If reasonable people can agree that the legacy model of publishing is an oligopoly (a market structure in which a few firms dominate), then an equally reasonable question might be what distinguishes academic publishing from a cartel (a form of oligopoly in which members collude to fix prices and production)? Whether or not the legacy scholarly publishing system meets the legal definition of a cartel, the legacy model of scholarly publishing – with its large profits for commercial publishers – has created a cost crisis for college and university libraries.

Serials crisis

Librarians have occasionally resisted the rising costs of scholarly journals and the duplicative, unnecessary purchases imposed on them by canceling certain of the 'big deal' packages. This generates alarm among students, faculty, and administrators, who develop familiarity with the interfaces that the publishers and distributors provide for online journal users. 'I need the EBSCO databases like I need air or water!' said one panicked Louisiana State University graduate student when she learned that one of her library's resources containing approximately 63,000 full-text electronic resources was threatened by rising subscription costs and declining budgets (Scudellari, 2010).

For the big five commercial publishers, the move to digital publication has not translated into real openness but into increased profits at the expense of what university libraries can afford to offer their constituents. This has created a serials crisis – a crisis driven not by the rising costs of publishing, but rather by the drive for profit by academic publishers. The switch to digital formats from print actually lowers distribution costs. Yet, as more and more academic journals have migrated to digital formats, publishers have dramatically raised subscription costs, and reduced flexibility and efficiency in journal distribution. In fact, prices for library journal subscriptions have risen at significantly greater rates than have indexes of consumer prices. North American research libraries' expenditures on journals increased 402% between 1986 and 2011 (Kryllidou et al, 2012); the average yearly cost for a library to subscribe to an academic journal in 2015 was over $1,933 (Bosch and Henderson, 2015). In the UK, journal expenditures account for over 65% of library budgets (*The Economist*, 2011). Journal costs in the science, technology, and medical fields increased most dramatically, but humanities and social sciences literature also consumed an increasingly greater portion of library budgets.

It seems counterintuitive. The costs of digital production are down (after initial outlay), but subscription prices are up. One factor to consider in that problematic trend is that publishers set prices in a market with reliable demand for singular, unique products. As academics have come to rely on the always available access to a current selection of core scholarly journals, commercial publishers may see an opportunity to profit and to proliferate subscriptions with 'big deal' package pricing structures. Purchase of only the top thirty journals in a field, for example, may be offered at a price comparable to a package that contains those thirty core titles, plus one thousand other less prestigious, but nonetheless potentially interesting journal titles. A la carte subscriptions to core journal titles are often discouraged or even disallowed, as publishers tend to market bundles of journals in most subject areas. According to analysis published in the *Proceedings of the National Academy of Sciences*, there is 'ample evidence that large publishers practice price discrimination and that they have been able to set prices well above average costs' (Bergstrom et al, 2014).

Periodical literature is the lifeblood of research scholarship ('like air or water'), so it is difficult for universities to resist paying publishers what they demand for key titles that academics rely upon. Staggering increases in subscription costs have coincided with, in some cases, equally staggering decreases in public funding for colleges and universities, and for their library collection budgets.

Resistance to the 'big deal' journal package subscriptions sometimes involves large-scale journal and database cancellations by college and university libraries. More often, it takes the form of scaled back or 'title-by-title' selective purchasing in a rejection of publishers' 'big deal' packages. Most academic libraries cannot afford to provide access to the fullest complement of a growing body of academic journal literature packaged in the 'big deal', and it is the cancellations, not the more pervasive failures of libraries to acquire the full range of academic titles, that grab headlines and academic attention. For instance, in 2010 New Mexico State University library announced the cancelation of more than 700 journal and database subscriptions; the University of California at San Francisco canceled 118 print and 115 online subscriptions; and the University of Washington announced cuts of 1,600 print and electronic journals (Scudellari, 2010). While librarians make adjustments to serials budgets all the time, the serials crisis causes concern for academic researchers. 'With a diminished library, you have a diminished university. It's that simple', says Robert Buckingham, Dean of the School of Public Health at the University of Saskatchewan (Scudellari, 2010).

It is not only the publicly funded institutions that are scaling back their journal subscriptions. Socially and fiscally responsible administrators at richly endowed Harvard University critique academic journal publishers for creating an untenable situation that is 'fiscally unsustainable' (Sample, 2012). Wealthy universities, too, as well as the lesser-funded public institutions are well invested in resisting publishers' rising costs and forging new models for scholarly communication.

It was a response to the serials crisis that jump-started the open access movement in the 1990s, spearheaded by academic library leaders (Oakerson and O'Donnell, 1995; Case, 1999; Shulenburger, 1999). In 1998, the Association of Research Libraries developed the Scholarly Publishing and Academic Resources Coalition (SPARC) to hasten the shift from the commercially based legacy system to open access that distributes publishing costs (not profits) equitably and efficiently among academic institutions, societies, funders, and publishers. SPARC is now 'a global coalition committed to making open the default for research and education', with over 800 member institutions in North America, Europe, Japan, China, and Australia.[1]

While it is not yet clear which models of open access scholarship will map to which disciplines on which sectors of the globe, it is increasingly clear that our legacy system of scholarly publishing – with its hyperinflating costs and its closed, inequitable, profit-driven patterns of distribution – is incompatible with the goals of its authors, universities, and scholarly societies, all of whom favor distributing academic work as widely as possible.

In 2012, Tim Gowers, a University of Cambridge mathematician frustrated by paywalls preventing intellectual access, wrote a blog post declaring that he would no longer submit to or review papers for any academic journal published by Elsevier (Gowers, 2012). Shortly afterward, one of Gowers' readers set up *The Cost of Knowledge* (an online petition where academics signed on to a similar declaration of non-support for Elsevier, with over 16,000 signatories as of this writing) (Neylon, 2012). Gowers' blog post, and the people who stand with him, were part of the movement known as the 'Academic Spring' of 2012, named after the Arab Spring movement that took off in 2011. Debates that escalated during the Academic Spring continue to shape thinking about the role of commercial interests in higher education (Jha, 2012). For instance, in 2015, Dutch universities threatened an all-out national boycott of Elsevier for its pricing practices (Kingsley and Harnad, 2015). But profiteering commercial publishers are not alone in creating this crisis; scholarly societies and associations shoulder some of the responsibility here, too.

Scholarly societies and associations

Scholarly societies and associations have come to rely heavily on the financial return provided to them by commercial publishers. Every discipline – from the Association of Art Historians to the International Society of Zoological Sciences – has at least one professional organization (sometimes more), to which scholars pay a membership fee. When scholars pay their membership dues, they gain access to the society's journals (typically behind paywalls) and often, they also gain a discounted admission fee to society-sponsored conferences.

Scholarly societies, like many institutions in the landscape of higher education, have been hit hard by austerity budgets, if somewhat indirectly. While universities once often covered association membership fees for faculty, it is no longer common practice. Today, membership fees generally come out of personal, household budgets rather than institutional budgets. As fewer scholars enter the ranks of the tenured or tenure track, there are simply fewer fully employed faculty with the kind of personal budgets that allow for association membership fees. For these reasons and others, membership in scholarly societies is on the decline at the same time as societies face rising costs (Fitzpatrick, 2012).

In this breach, scholarly societies have welcomed the expanding role of commercial entities – publishers and content providers such as JSTOR, Project Muse, ProQuest, and others – to manage the production and distribution of scholarly work. Publishers and content providers strike deals with the struggling associations to share in the profits from the production or distribution of the discipline's journals. Thus, the interests of scholarly societies become aligned with those of their scholarly production outsourcers – Elsevier, Springer, Wiley, Taylor & Francis, and Sage. Most associations and societies adhere closely to the standard contracts with commercial publishers for the revenue it generates for them, and the labor and expertise it spares them. Some academics fear that sticking to these production and distribution patterns may destroy the associations (Best, 2015). Others worry that any change to the legacy model of publishing, and societies' stake in it, will have dreadful consequences. Open access and elimination of a library-funded subscription revenue stream may exacerbate the financial distress that publishers fear, and thereby threaten to destabilize many of their partner societies (Shieber, 2013). But lost in this calculation is the societies' primary goal of sharing scholarly work as widely and as publicly as possible, because the associations' perceived economic interests militate against it.

While publishers' profit-making in scholarly communication must decidedly evolve or decline, open access need not spell the end of scholarly societies. According to an analysis of the tax returns for 20 scholarly associations in the US, a switch to open access would actually help their bottom line. This study suggested that societies could make up the loss of a revenue stream sacrificed for an open access model through cost savings and other revenue sources. At the same time, associations implementing open access would better serve their membership by increasing readership (Willinsky, 2004). Digital technologies provide lower barriers to publishing and to open access distribution, but societies remain hesitant to publish and to distribute journals without engaging outside entities to manage it. The labor required to shift established journals to open access models is significant, and open access does not come without start-up, infrastructure, and maintenance costs.

However, a number of editorial boards have resigned in 'journal declarations of independence' from working with commercial publishers, in order to pursue publication with less restrictive access policies (OA Community, 2016). Many of these declarations are made in direct protest against the commercial publishers. For instance, in 2015 the entire editorial staff at *Lingua*, a leading journal in linguistics, resigned in protest over Elsevier's policies and decided to launch their own, open access version of the journal (Moody, 2015; see also www.wired.co.uk/article/elsevier-versus-open-access, but note the point of clarification at the bottom of the page). Anne-Marie Tessler, a professor of linguistics and one of the editors who resigned from *Lingua*, explained what it was like trying to get fellow academics to review for a journal published by Elsevier:

> You reach out to people and say, "Can you review this paper for *Lingua*?" Increasingly people said, "Honestly, I'm not willing to review for *Lingua* or submit work there anymore because I don't think it's reasonable to support a model where the research winds up so monetized". (Samson, 2015)

But it was really the desire to move the journal to a fully (gold) open access model that created the impasse. Under their contract, the only way for articles to be openly available was for authors to pay a fee. Tessler explained it this way:

> ... [the] Elsevier model is that if you, as an author, want your specific article to be open access then you or someone backing you – an institution or a granting agency – has to pony up €1,800. For one article! It's really beyond the means of almost any individual author. (Samson, 2015)

Tessler also mentioned that several people reported that because of the high subscription costs, their institutions were no longer going to be able to subscribe to *Lingua*. That means, Tessler says, 'we've lost the plot. This is no longer a viable method for research dissemination if we have to bargain as to which of the journals we're going to be able to subscribe to' (Samson, 2015). The larger point, that this is 'no longer a viable method of research dissemination', is true not only for individual journals such as *Lingua*, but also for entire fields of scholarship.

'We must stop arguing for or against OA in terms of the difference it makes as a publishing rationale for this or that journal', contend the editors of *Cultural Anthropology*, the recently launched open access journal of the American Anthropological Association (Jiménez et al, 2015). 'There is more at stake than the long-term sustainability of any one individual publication. If there is one thing clear at this stage, it is that OA demands a collective and inventive redefinition of the ecology of scholarly publishing', they argue.

These editors note that anthropology owns its own journals as a 'common property resource', unlike many social science and humanities disciplines where the most prestigious journal titles have become the property of commercial publishers. This position allows anthropology to collectively 'redefine the future of scholarly publishing' (Jiménez et al, 2015). Thinking collectively about scholarly publishing shifts our focus from the viability of any one journal to reconsidering the taken-for-granted relationships among scholarly associations, their members, and commercial publishers.

Legacy models of scholarly publishing – with hyperinflating costs and closed and inequitable patterns of distribution – serve the interests of publishers and content providers distributing to libraries for high subscription prices more keenly than the interests of globally networked scholars (Stewart, 2015).

Scholarly books and monographs

The legacy model of academic book publishing operates in a different, but not entirely distinct, ecosystem from that of journal publishing. University presses and small independent presses were created in the 19th century, when people recognized that scholarly work would languish if left to the vagaries of the market (Abel et al, 2002). From the perspective of commercial publishers at that time, the potential audience for most academic work was too small, and hence the costs to publishers too high, to turn a profit. However, even among commercial publishers, there was a recognition that knowledge would be lost if the marketplace were the only arbiter for academic publication. 'What is accomplished if the work of a lifetime grows moldy in the drawer of a desk?' asked Charles Scribner, a commercial publisher and a founder of Princeton University Press (Hawes, 1967, p. 35). Innovators in the 19th century proposed that the university should take on the job of publication itself (Abel et al, 2002). So, university presses were formed to support the university in disseminating the knowledge it was charged with creating.

University presses often also publish scholarly journals. As of 2002, there were 92 university presses in the United States and Canada (Abel et al, 2002). Among them they publish approximately 11,000 books each year, and over 700 peer-reviewed journals. Traditionally, scholars in the humanities and social sciences have relied on university presses to publish their books and monographs intended for small audiences of other experts. University presses have been long pressured to operate under a cost recovery model. The most recent recession and deeper austerity have cut editorial staff, decreased the acquisition of new titles, and in some cases forced presses to merge with university libraries. The range of traditional publishing options diminishes at the same time as the array of digital publishing opportunities expands.

Textbooks

Textbook authoring is one of the few arenas of the legacy model of scholarship that pays. A textbook that is widely adopted can provide academic authors with a very handsome income from royalties. While this system works for successful textbook authors, it works against their students. The benefits that authors derive are directly and literally at the expense of their undergraduate readers. Many students simply don't buy required books because they cannot afford them. One researcher found that 65% of students opted against buying textbooks because they were too costly (Grasgreen, 2014). Of those, 94% were concerned that their grades would suffer because of it.

The price of textbooks has risen 812% since 1978, with the average price of a textbook settling somewhere around $68 in 2012 (Otani, 2015). The College Board in 2015-16 advised students attending US public two-year institutions to budget a whopping $1,364 for books and supplies (College Board, 2016). Learning and education are not promoted by high textbook costs.

Digital scholarship and many paths to open access

Digital scholarship, in which opening, moving, remixing, sharing, and circulating information are core practices, offers many paths to open access. Innovation in digital scholarship has already demonstrated that there is an audience for the work that academics create.

'What we're seeing is that the general public wants to read scholarly papers', says Richard Price, founder of Academia.edu, an Internet start-up that describes itself as a 'platform for academics to share research papers' (McKenna, 2015). This company has come under fire from academics around the question, as Kathleen Fitzpatrick put it, of 'What will become of their work in the long term?' Her concern is that a start-up, funded by venture capital (as Academia.edu is), will eventually find a way to show a profit. To do that, they may monetize the content on their site or sell user-generated data from it. That is, they will have to use the academic work posted there in ways that the authors of that work never intended. Fitzpatrick also finds it problematic that this for-profit company uses the '.edu' domain name, potentially confusing users. Open access is 'good for the public and good for the researchers', Fitzpatrick says, but she believes that a commercial platform like Academia.edu is the wrong place for academics to share their work (Fitzpatrick, 2015). But this controversy leaves many academics befuddled about what to do if they want to share their work openly.

Platforms like Academia.edu do not solve the problems with the broader ecology of the legacy model of scholarly publishing. Academics continue to be under-informed about how open access and self-archiving work. In 2014, Elsevier sent Academia.edu users hundreds of take-down notices, alerting unaware authors who had published with Elsevier that they were violating their publishing agreements by posting their articles on the site. In fact, scholars often do violate copyright agreements with their publishers when they share work on the site as well as on others. For now, Elsevier has stopped demanding that authors who post their work at Academia.edu in violation of Elsevier contracts take the work down. But confusion persists for many academics, both about what their individual obligations to publishers are and about the general open access terrain. To understand both the restrictions on one's own scholarly work and the current landscape of scholarly publishing, it is important to understand the difference between two going models of open access: 'gold open access' and 'green open access', and the 'hybrid' publishing models with qualities of both legacy publishing and open access.

Gold open access: perpetually open for non-paying readers

Gold open access journals are those that publish exclusively without subscription or reader charges, producing peer-reviewed articles that are perpetually open for non-paying readers from the moment of publication. While the journals from several successful gold open access journal portals – including Brazil's *SciELO*,[2] Mexico's *Readalyc*,[3] and *African Journals Online*[4] – do not require authors to finance publication of their research, the majority of gold open access journals based in the global North require authors (or most often their funding agencies) to pay publishing charges to support the journals.

Author publishing charges (APCs) vary widely by discipline and by publisher. The more prominent science, technology, and math journals charge APCs that shock those in the less well-funded social sciences and humanities. For example, perhaps the most well-known open access journals, the Public Library of Science (PLoS) series, charges authors between $1,350 and $2,900 per article. Springer BioMed Central requires fees of between $735 and $2,605.[5]

The author-funded gold open access model of scholarly publishing has the unintended consequence of generating opportunities for deceptive practices. Scammers, posing as reputable academic journal editors, have been successful in soliciting articles for bogus journals and conferences in order to pocket fees without offering anything in return. Unsuspecting authors may be taken in by increasingly sophisticated calls to publish papers in open access journals, only to find that the payment resulted in nothing that resembles the practice of scholarly publishing. That is, scholarly peers do not review the paper and it is neither substantively edited nor copyedited. Or, a potential author may find that upon payment of a hefty fee, an article fails to appear in any form whatsoever. Clearly, it is possible for unscrupulous actors other than commercial publishers to profit from APCs that are standard operating procedure under the gold open access model.

To counter this offense, the Directory of Open Access Journals (DOAJ), the foremost index of reputable peer review open access journals (see Box 4.1), moved in 2015 to expand its description of open access journal features to identify deceptive publishers or to eliminate them from its listing. DOAJ provides a set of quality and functional standards for gold open access journal producers (DOAJ, 2015). Still, academic authors must remain vigilant about the risk of being separated from their money in an APC scam, just as we watch for unscrupulous 'vanity' publishers who seek to profit from print-based scholarship without providing adequate review or distribution.

Commercial journal publishers – Elsevier, Springer, Wiley, Taylor & Francis and Sage – have each developed 'hybrid' publishing options that offer readers open access in subscription-based journals, supported by APCs. The hybrid models preserve and even increase publisher revenue, while doing little to shift the landscape of scholarly publishing to one that is open, affordable, and accessible. The way it works is as follows: authors publish in a traditional journal (that libraries pay publishers to subscribe to), but they can opt to pay an extra fee (averaging between $3,000 and $5,000) for an article to be made available immediately as gold open access (Larivière et al, 2015). In some instances, 'immediate gold open access' is required by a funding mandate. For example, funding organizations such as the Wellcome Trust in the UK, the National Institutes of Health in the US, the Canadian Institute of Health, and the European Research Council require research to be available upon publication. In such circumstances, authors must select their publishers with these parameters in mind.

In other instances, researchers are under no such mandate. After a waiting period (called an 'embargo'), publishers and/or funders often make an article openly available through a public platform, such as PubMed. Authors often need do nothing, and pay no APC, for the work to eventually become open access; publishers do the posting for the authors when their embargo period expires. However, author uncertainty about these processes can pose an opportunity for scammers to collect false APCs. This nearly happened to me (Daniels), when I received an email from what I thought was a professional association (the American Public Health Association), asking me if I wanted to make an article I had published with a traditional publisher 'open access' for a mere $3,000. The article had been published for a year in the association's leading journal, *American Journal of Public Health*, and it was already available through PubMed.[6]

With APCs now commonplace and accepted by funders and authors alike, commercial publishers of open access content have not significantly shifted their legacy journal publishing business model. Publishers continue to thrive at the expense of the academic authors, reviewers, readers and their libraries, who spend at an increasing collective rate to not only protect but also actually to increase publisher profits. Springer bought BioMed Central in 2008, and by 2015 Springer had become the largest open access publisher of academic work. These efforts to encourage open access risk further concentrating the control of academic publishing within a few powerful institutions (Brienza, 2015). While the gold open access model that relies on charging authors currently functions for well-funded science, technology, and math scholars in the global North, it is not workable for the humanities and social sciences, and just about any underfunded scholar, including many in the global South.

This move toward the 'default' open position for scholarship also means that research conducted by, and data conducted about, oppressed peoples and communities might be compelled by funding agencies to open to public readership. Data and scholarship open to scrutiny and reuse by audiences hostile to, or untrained in, analysis may be applied to support narratives and analysis counter to those forwarded by the producers.

Open scholarship does not necessarily lead a steady march toward one truth or vision. Open scholarship, and the debate about it, bears the certainty of messy understandings, confusion, conflict, misappropriation, and tangential focus. But, it is only in this open sphere that scholarship has any power and potential at all to engage debate and to shift understandings. Open scholarship can generate counter-narrative, but only open scholarship can re-engage that counter-narrative as well. Open scholarship assumes a faith in the power of rationality.

Green open access: pre-print, do it yourself, self-archiving

'Green open access' is author self-archiving, and it is available now. It requires more work from an individual author, but no author charges are imposed. Green open access allows authors to post a version of their article on their own website or an institutional repository, or even on a commercial platform. This is called 'self-archiving', because the author takes action to archive the paper. Self-archived works are discoverable in varying degrees by Internet search engines and freely accessible to any reader on the web. These works can be downloaded by readers without encountering a paywall.

The 'pre-print' version of the article, the version that publishers commonly allow authors to self-archive, is typically the last revision that the researcher sent to the publisher before it is printed in the journal.[7] Some journals allow publication in a traditional journal with self-archiving at the same time. Other journals require an embargo period of 6 to 18 months between the time an article is published in a journal and the time publishers permit it to be self-archived. During the embargo period, the publisher is the exclusive distributor of the work. Once the publisher's embargo period is reached, researchers may deposit a copy of their work with an open access institutional repository, a subject-based repository, or a personal web page.

Embargoes are often levied in combination with further conditions that the author not openly archive the peer-reviewed or the publisher's final version of an article, but instead the author must post a pdf version of the article derived from the author's files. Other publishers do the opposite, and stipulate, for example, that a self-archived article must retain the journal publisher's format. Some publishers ask that final works reflecting the peer review and editing they direct not be shared with open access readers; only the pre-prints or non-peer review versions of a published work are authorized by these publishers to be publicly archived. It is also the case that publishers rarely record the revisions of an article as it approaches publication, and the collaborative nature of the process makes it difficult to differentiate among reviewer-directed revisions and author-determined revisions. Authors often claim the final revised versions as their own without ruffling publisher feathers. Publishers who quibble may issue take-down notices, as Elsevier did with self-archived work on the Academia.edu platform.

Green open access allows authors greater flexibility about where to publish, and it maintains publishers' positions as sole distributors of new academic work. With this, it preserves incentives for libraries to continue to subscribe to academic journals. Green open access preserves publishers' legacy roles as exclusive distributors of current content, while shifting the archiving responsibilities to authors and to institutional repositories, which are often university libraries. Like gold open access, green open access does not immediately challenge publisher profits or the legacy model of journal publishing, but it promotes an evolution toward open access platforms. Green open access also engages a shift toward self-conscious archival practice on the part of authors to preserve scholarship and to keep it freely and widely available in present and future digital contexts.

Publishers have responded to green open access initiatives with a variety of terms and conditions for self-archiving, mostly designed to shore up publishers' exclusive right to distribute new research. Some publishers have lengthened embargoes as green open access archiving has gained steam. Funders influence the length of time publishers may embargo research from public access by mandating public access for the research they fund within specific periods of time.

As of this writing, green open access is accepted by a majority of journals and their publishers. Of 2,175 leading academic journal publishers around the world, 78% formally permit authors to self-archive their work as a matter of standing policy (SHERPA/RoMEO, 2016). Of the 22% of publishers lacking formal support for green open access, some explicitly comply with author-initiated requests to self-archive by revising publishing contracts, and still others will not explicitly object nor issue take-down notices when authors post their own archival work on the open web.

Authors can usually find the specifics of a publisher's self-archiving policies in the agreements they sign for publication. But these documents are dense, and eyes understandably glaze over at the 'tl/dr' (too long, didn't read) nature of these contracts. The SHERPA/RoMEO toolset offers an alternative to this tedium (see Box 4.2). Here, anyone can type in the title of a journal and immediately find a clear, easy-to-understand description of that publication's self-archiving – or green open access – policies.

While green open access allows motivated scholars to make their work available to global publics immediately and comprehensively, it is a less than perfect fix for the wide-ranging change that our scholarly publishing system requires. Its reliance on individual scholars to place their own work in an online archive in combination with rules that publishers impose is an impediment to the widest possible distribution of research.

Our discussion thus far has centered on journal literature, in part because this is where the greatest crisis in scholarly publishing lies, and because this is where most of the advocacy around open access has been focused. The rise in digital scholarship has also begun to shift the discussion of publishing scholarly books.

The Open Access Network: a viable model for change

How do we move from a legacy system of scholarly publishing to one that is open, scalable, and sustainable? On the one hand, many universities and their libraries now support institutional repositories where pre-prints can be deposited for green open access, as well as home-grown open journal publishing programs. On the other hand, publishers affiliated with some scholarly societies and university presses are promoting gold open access options for their journals and books. But these open funding models have not yet changed the publishing landscape significantly enough to herald an all-out shift in the scholarly communications infrastructure. 'We need a sustainable system for scholarship writ large', writes librarian and blogger Barbara Fister (2016).

Rebecca Kennison and Lisa Norberg, co-founders of the Open Access Network (OAN), contend that professional societies, universities, and academic publishers need to realign their relationship and work together to transform the scholarly communication infrastructure (Kennison and Norberg, 2014). The model they propose takes an incremental or phased approach, opening up current forms of scholarship (for example journals, monographs), while simultaneously establishing the infrastructure necessary to build, support, and sustain new and emerging modes of communication. They focus on publications and platforms in disciplines in the humanities and social sciences, which are most at risk in the current cost-per-unit-driven open access environment.

The financial model behind the proposed OAN involves an annual or multi-year payment made by every institution of higher education, based on a sliding scale tied to the institution's classification. In the US, that is set by the Carnegie Classification of Institutions of Higher Education,[8] and outside the US it is the International Standard Classification of Education.[9] The payment would be many factors smaller than what most institutions currently pay for journal subscriptions (K|N Consultants, 2016). But pooled together, this funding would be enough to support a robust infrastructure for scholarly publishing.

This reimagined, though still unrealized, approach embodies the kind of systemic thinking and ambition needed to make large-scale change. 'From creation and innovation of new publishing platforms to preservation of the record,' Kennison and Norberg's OAN is 'working out a map for how to build and sustain new kinds of publishing that meet the needs of all stakeholders through collaboration and a commitment to openness,' Barbara Fister writes (Fister, 2016).

The OAN model that Kennison and Norberg proposes aims to meet the needs of a variety of stakeholders, including scholars, professional societies, universities, and academic publishers. If adopted, their proposal would realign a complex set of relationships within scholarly communication infrastructure to create and preserve the scholarly record. To be sure, our current system of scholarly communication is broken. It will take inspired, ambitious efforts such as OAN to fix it.

Open access books, monographs and textbooks

'I didn't write this book to make money', reveals danah boyd (who spells her name with lower case letters), of her book, *It's complicated*, about teenagers' social lives on and off the Internet (boyd, 2014a). 'I don't actually care whether or not my book _sells_ a lot; I care whether or not it's _read_ a lot' (boyd, 2014b). What boyd says she cared most about was getting the widest possible audience for her work and 'this desire to get as many people as engaged as possible drove every decision I made throughout this process'. One of the decisions she made was to publish with Yale University Press explicitly because of their willingness to let her put a freely downloadable copy of the book online on the day the book came out. She did just that. The day her book was published, she also posted a pdf of the entire book on her own website.

Her experience with publishing her book may be different from the traditional academic's experience, but then that might be expected, as danah boyd is not a traditional academic. She is well regarded among those who study the Internet and works outside academia as a Principal Researcher at Microsoft. In 2014, boyd launched her own research and think tank, Data & Society, to bring attention to the way the algorithms that undergird big data affect society, and conversely, the way inequalities in society shape the algorithms that get coded. The appearance of digitally fluent, hybrid scholars, like danah boyd, who are more interested in reach and impact on a broader public than in climbing the academic career ladder, point to a different approach to being a scholar, one that is rooted in public engagement and activism. These scholars are less inclined than previous generations to publish scholarly monographs that only two hundred people will ever read.

Despite shifting priorities of scholars like boyd, book publishers still have to confront the vicissitudes of the marketplace. There is some evidence to suggest that sales of print form books can remain strong when books are available online for free (T. Anderson, 2013). One study even found an *increase* in print sales after release of free online versions (Hilton III and Wiley, 2010). Increasingly, book publishers are experimenting with providing online versions of texts as enticements to buy the long form in print (Eve, 2014). For her part, danah boyd says that she wanted to encourage people to buy the book, even though there was a free version available online, because 'when people purchase the book, they signal to outside folks that the book is important' (boyd, 2014b).

Viewing scholarly publishing through a social justice lens

'Open Access is, perhaps above all other things, a moral and political decision', observe Jiménez and colleagues (Jiménez et al, 2015). Clearly, one of us (Thistlethwaite) got this message from participating in ACT

UP, as described at the beginning of this chapter. This idea did not become salient for me (Daniels) until much more recently.

During a live radio interview shortly after my book *Cyber racism* (2009) came out, a young man called in to confront me. His was not the usual angry response I tend to receive in doing such work, either from white supremacists on the far right who call me 'libtard' (among other names), or from those on the center-left who find my critical focus on racism upsetting to their notions of colorblindness. Instead, he was angry because I had, a few days prior to this, asked him to remove a pirated copy of my book that he had posted on his website. I believed I was doing the right thing when I contacted the blogging platform he used and reported him for hosting an unauthorized e-version of my book that anyone could download. Then, he asked me this crucial question: 'Why are you doing this work? Don't you want people who can least afford it to read your work?' His question prompted me to reevaluate my relationship to copyright and whose interests it served.

After this encounter, I began to realize that my attempt to enforce my publisher's copyright protection for the book was serving the interests of the publisher more than it was serving my own goals for the book. In an ironic twist, when I submitted my materials for tenure and promotion, the requirements stipulated that I include six copies of all my publications, including my two books. To do this, I had to go to an online commercial retailer, buy six copies of each book (approximately $450) in order to apply for a promotion at my own institution. It had never been clearer to me that I no longer owned my own work.

It was several years later, through working on JustPublics@365 (see Chapter Two), that I began to see open access as connected to other social justice issues. What was the point, I asked myself, of doing this work if no one could read it? It was the first time that I questioned what I had been told and what I understood about scholarly publishing, and I began to apply a sociological analysis to it.

The justifications and explanations for what we call the legacy model of publishing were, like those for any other ideology, meant to disguise economic interests, but once you start to pull on one thread the whole thing begins to unravel. At the same time, it was becoming more and more evident to both of us (and to many others) that digital technologies had the potential to transform scholarly communication.

Our experiments with open access

Throughout the many facets of our project, we wanted to experiment with what scholarly communication could be if it were truly open and informed by social justice goals. To do this, we tried to advance open access in multiple ways, through a series of eBooks tied to the summits and through the participatory, open, online course (POOC) (see Chapters Two and Three).

Social justice series of eBooks as continuous publishing

'Continuous publishing', a term coined by Mark Carrigan, author of *Social media for academics* (2016a), is a way of thinking about knowledge creation in the digital era. 'With this approach one's social media presence becomes something like a public notebook, drawing together ongoing research activity in a way which invites others to respond and participate' (Carrigan, 2016b).

When we were reimagining the academic conference as a summit that connected scholars, activists, journalists, and documentary filmmakers, we also wanted to re-envision knowledge production from academic conferences. To do this, we created a companion eBook on the same topic as each of the summits (see Chapter Two). In a way, the series of eBooks we created were an extension of Carrigan's notion of 'continuous publishing'. We wanted to take the social media in and around the events, as well as curated and invited content after the events, and compile them into eBooks. For us, it represented a collaborative and born-digital model of knowledge production.

The finished eBooks that we produced became open educational resources (OERs). In the contemporary lexicon of higher education, OER refers to a wide range of open access items, like the ones we included in our series and compiled into an eBook, that can be used for student learning. For faculty who want to help eliminate the student burden of textbook costs, OERs are a compelling choice. For example, the Commonwealth of Learning's Directory of Open Educational Resources provides textbook alternatives for higher education and technical training, arranged by subject and learning level (DOER, 2016). We created the eBooks as ways to reimagine scholarly communication, knowledge creation, and activism, but they are now used in college classes as open access texts.

Our other experiment with open access was connected to our participatory, open, online course (POOC), #InQ13 (discussed in Chapter Three).

Open access course materials for community engagement

Making the readings for #InQ13 fully open to anyone on the web who wanted to participate was a primary goal of launching the course. The course was focused on a specific New York City neighborhood and was designed to engage community members. We knew we could not do that if all the readings, or really any of them, were blocked and required university logins to access. What not all of us realized at the outset is that this would require a great deal of work from a rather large and collaborative team, but one with divisions of labor and responsibility. These divisions of labor, fuzzy at first, became clearer as the course progressed. In a conventional legacy model course, one instructor selects readings to teach a small group of students. In this unique participatory course, a 20-member team was required to *produce* the course, with two instructors, for thousands of students, both enrolled at the Graduate Center and not enrolled, participating from geographically dispersed locations (Daniels et al, 2014). While everyone involved in the project embraced the concept of open access as a laudable goal, at the beginning none of us were experienced in the mechanics of open access discovery, identification, permission seeking, and posting.

In most courses, the instructor is the sole arbiter of course readings, but making sure all the readings for #InQ13 were open access was an elaborately collaborative process. The #InQ13 course instructors Wendy Luttrell and Caitlin Cahill provided an initial 'wish list' of readings in the usual way and without regard to licensing restrictions. This list, for 14 class sessions, totaled 117 articles, book chapters, websites, blogs, films, and entire books. I (Daniels), along with the production team, reviewed the syllabus. Following that and in conversation with instructors, together we found or forged open access equivalents for 47 titles, or about 40% of the traditionally licensed required readings. Librarians (Thistlethwaite and Smith-Cruz) then reviewed the remaining list to examine the licensing status of the readings and to determine what steps the team might take to obtain key readings in open access formats. Librarians reviewed journal articles and, fortunately, several authors had self-archived the pieces, so anyone in the 'class', meaning anyone at all, could get to them. Books and films required publisher (or other rights-holder) permissions and cooperation (Smith-Cruz et al, 2014).

Community members as copyright owners

Our librarian–author collaboration proved to be compelling to publishers. Librarians contacted book publishers, copying in authors, lecturers, and course organizers on all correspondence, about making their work open to all who wanted to participate in the course. Many authors were honored to have their work included and volunteered to contact publishers via personal correspondence. A few of the publishers we contacted (three out of 19) understood the nature of our request and responded positively to offer publications openly, for a limited period of time. Some of the other publishers we contacted responded but declined our invitation to participate; others simply never responded at all. The three academic publishers that allowed temporary open online posting for the #InQ13 course were University of California (UC) Press, New York University (NYU) Press, and University of Minnesota (UMN) Press.

UC Press posted the introduction and chapter three of Dávila's (2004) *Barrio dreams: Puerto Ricans, Latinos, and the neoliberal city*; prior to our request, the press had featured the book's introduction on its website, as a way to entice readers to buy the book. UC also posted two chapters of Pulido, Barraclough, and Cheng's (2012) *A people's guide to Los Angeles*; and chapter five of Wilson Gilmore's (2007) *Golden gulag: prisons, surplus, crisis, and opposition in globalizing California*.

NYU Press provided Londono's chapter 'Aesthetic belonging: the Latinization & renewal of Union City, New Jersey' from the 2012 anthology *Latino urbanism: the politics of planning, policy, and redevelopment* (edited by Diaz and Torres).

UMN Press offered the biggest win as measured by the amount of text pages, posting the entirety of Katz's (2004) *Growing up global: economic restructuring and children's everyday lives* in downloadable pdf format through a link on the press's website. Publishers kept all links live from the time we reached agreement through to the end of the semester-long course.

Early in the term, #InQ13 course coordinators approached filmmaker Ed Morales about his 2008 documentary film, *Whose barrio? The gentrification of East Harlem*, requesting that he post it free online for the course's second module. Morales retains the copyright for his work, and he was also a guest participant in the course. He readily complied, posting his film to be viewed free, open, and online via his own platform, which he maintains through the Internet Movie Database. Morales' eager participation was early inspiration to organizers, who went forward to convince other authors and publishers to make their work openly available.

Another instance produced a thornier result. One course lecturer believed that she retained copyright of her forthcoming book. She assured course organizers that the publisher's correspondence confirmed permission to post chapters on the course website. However, librarians' end-of-course review of the email correspondence revealed a misinterpretation of the publisher's correspondence. The publisher had in fact withheld permission to post the work. The posted chapters were removed from the temporary course repository when we discovered the error.

Yet a different book publisher responded with a course pack license agreement requesting a fee to permit 57 pages to be copied no more than 20 times. While the initial letter to the publisher had been clear about the nature of the open, online course, the author's appearance as a guest lecturer, and the request that the material be made free to any reader on the web, the publisher either misunderstood the request or was at a loss as to how to respond. Upon clarifying this issue, the publisher was willing to negotiate a license and fee to allow online distribution of two requested chapters, but only if distribution could be limited to a specified number of students. A subsequent attempt to communicate with this publisher went unanswered.

Two tools proved essential for reviewing course readings: the Directory of Open Access Journals[10] and the SHERPA/RoMEO tool[11] (see Boxes 4.1 and 4.2). More than 32,000 scholarly periodicals are included in these two tools. Applying both DOAJ and SHERPA/RoMEO to the course lists, we soon discovered lots of rogue postings, scholarly articles or book chapters posted online without regard for publishers' restrictions or the author's wishes. We also learned that while author self-archiving is *allowed* by hundreds of traditional academic publishers, this option was at the time (2013) not widely exercised by authors. Through ongoing conversations with librarians and faculty involved in our project, authors inevitably became aware of, and in some cases expert in, publishers' policies as it applied to their work. This awareness was a good step forward, but an incremental one, to be sure.

Forward thinking: acting like opening up knowledge matters

It is impossible to be a scholar in the digital age without considering open access to knowledge. Too often, scholars who have the privilege of university access forget that many others are locked out of the databases we take for granted. We may even scoff at the idea that our work might have value beyond the academy, but as Sarah Kendzior points out (Tadween Editors, 2013), this is an elitist position. We never know who might consider our work meaningful or what kind of use they might find for it.

What is exciting about the emergence of digital technologies for all kinds of scholars is that they offer the promise of openness to all kinds of knowledge. Yet the legacy model of publishing chokes this potential. While the legacy model of publishing offers scholars a reliable form of credentialing, it is broken in many other ways. For readers outside the academy, paywalls make it almost impossible to engage with scholarly writing, should they want to do so. The serials crisis is choking library budgets and textbooks are so expensive that many students cannot afford to buy them. Yet, the legacy model of publishing works quite well for the big five commercial publishers. It also works to the benefit of some scholarly societies and associations, at least for now. But this broken system is beginning to fray at the edges as scholars begin to question its legitimacy.

Forward-thinking scholars, such as the editorial board of *Lingua* who resigned en masse and are starting a new, fully open access journal, are charting new paths to open access. Similarly, the principled editors of *Cultural Anthropology* are not only creating their own open access journal, but they are also pushing their scholarly association, the American Anthropological Association, to do more to rethink what they call 'the ecology of scholarly publishing' (Jiménez et al, 2015).

In our own experiment, we tried to further open access in several ways. We created social justice eBooks as open access companion artifacts to summits, as a form of 'continuous publishing' and as a way of extending and deepening the connections we enabled there. These had the unintended consequence of also being open educational resources. We also worked diligently to make all the readings in the #InQ13 course fully open for anyone who wanted to read them. Small, incremental steps, to be sure, but these are valuable for the possibilities that they suggest. Being a scholar in the digital era is an opportunity to imagine all that we could do if our scholarship were open and connected.

We began this chapter with the proposition that opening up knowledge matters. When we open the usual channels in which knowledge is created, we make collaborations possible. When we open education and link it to communities, we can learn from and strengthen the communities where our colleges and universities are located. When we create structures that make knowledge open to all, we encourage both democracy and innovation. This is a more just world than smuggling people into libraries to be able to read the latest medical research. It is partial answer to the question: Why are you doing this work?

Box 4.1: Directory of Open Access Journals

The Directory of Open Access Journals (DOAJ) (http://doaj.org), a list of and review mechanism for peer-reviewed OA journals, can help authors sort out whether or not a journal is a legitimate publisher of scholarly work or an exploitative venture. DOAJ's growth parallels the growth of gold OA journal publishing. Launched at Lund University, Sweden, in 2003 with 300 journals, in 2015 the DOAJ lists more than 10,000 OA journal titles. DOAJ is fueled by a small central staff and a host of volunteers and funded by voluntary membership and donation. Library content aggregators, such as ProQuest's Serial Solutions, Summon, and Primo, link from library abstracts to full text OA using metadata harvested from DOAJ. This means library article databases link to OA journal articles, and not only to subscription-based journals. In 2014 DOAJ introduced an expanded application form and review process to produce improved quality markers. These include, for example, the presence of a journal's article-level metadata, a journal's alignment with funder-mandated requirements, Creative Commons licensing policies, and the presence and level of APCs. These developments will expand DOAJ's scope significantly and increase its value to authors, publishers, and researchers.

BOX 4.2: SHERPA/RoMEO

SHERPA/RoMEO (www.sherpa.ac.uk/romeo/index.php) is a searchable database of publishers' general policies on journal article self-archiving. It provides a standardized, verified representation of the standing policies of over 22,000 peer-reviewed journals. Funded initially by the Wellcome Trust, and currently by JISC, and hosted by the University of Nottingham in the UK, RoMEO staff comb publishers' copyright agreements and online open access policies. They correspond with publishers to aggregate, standardize, and translate journal self-archiving policies into easy-to-understand, color coded categories to facilitate comparison of journal self-archiving policies. RoMEO is indispensible to green OA projects, facilitating compliance and collaboration among contributing authors, publishers, and repository managers.

Notes

[1] See sparcopen.org
[2] See www.scielo.br
[3] See www.redalyc.org
[4] See www.ajol.info
[5] Springer BioMed Central currently points to their gold OA journal APCs from www.biomedcentral.com/publishing-services/publication-costs-and-funding
[6] I wrote to the president of the association, telling him that this was a questionable practice. He promised to look into it and get back to me. I am still waiting for a reply.
[7] SHERPA/RoMEO can clarify which version of authors' works publishers allow to be self-archived.
[8] See http://carnegieclassifications.iu.edu/
[9] See www.uis.unesco.org/Education/Pages/international-standard-classification-of-education.aspx
[10] See https://doaj.org/
[11] See www.sherpa.ac.uk/romeo

FIVE

Training scholars for
the digital era

'To be a scholar is, often, to be irrelevant,' writes Nicholas Kristof in his op-ed (opinion editorial) column in the *New York Times* (Kristof, 2014b). 'Some of the smartest thinkers on problems at home and around the world are university professors, but most of them just don't matter in today's great debates.' Instead, he writes, professors are cloistered 'like medieval monks' (Kristof, 2014b).

His comments touched off a firestorm among scholars who are already using digital technologies to engage public audiences beyond the academy, including one who started a hashtag '#engagedacademics' in response to Kristof's column (Pearson, 2014). Much of the push back from academics involved some variation on the argument that Kristof needed to cast a wider net when looking for examples of academics engaging beyond the academy (Chenoweth, 2014). 'I gave a talk [on] the history of black education at my church this morning. Not sure if this is the kind of work @NickKristof wants ;)' tweeted Blair L. M. Kelly, a professor of history at North Carolina State University. Dozens of other academics made a similar point in more extended formats (Daniels, 2014). 'There are hundreds of academic political scientists whose research is far from irrelevant and who seek to communicate their insights to the general public via blogs, social media, op-eds, online lectures and so on. They are easier to find than ever before', responded Erik Voeten, on the *Washington Post* blog *Monkey Cage* (Voeten, 2014).

Part of Kristof's complaint is that academics spend far too much time publishing 'gobbledygook ... hidden in obscure journals' (Kristof, 2014b). Some academics responded that this was an old critique, little more than anti-intellectualism that amounted to a stereotype that 'all academics write badly' (Thomson, 2014). Kristof further elaborated his concerns in a follow-up blog post, 'Bridging the moat around universities' (Kristof, 2014a). The title is a play on Jill Lepore's description of academia: 'a great, heaping mountain of exquisite knowledge surrounded by a vast moat of dreadful prose' (Lepore, 2013). If only academics could bridge the moat between the university and wider publics by writing more clearly, Kristof urged. Kristof's lament echoes Russell Jacoby's mournful cry about the lack of plain writing a generation earlier in his book *The last intellectuals* (1987). This generation of academics has much more pressure to publish in order to survive in academia, and more than a few people faulted Kristof for not fully appreciating the pressure to publish in traditional academic journals.

'His column and subsequent blog post just seems so out-of-touch with the machine of the academy', writes Syreeta McFadden, an editor at *Union Station Magazine* and adjunct professor of English (McFadden, 2014). She points to the real-life economic interests that drive academics toward publishing, and these are linked to getting hired and promoted in the academy. 'People need jobs, my dude! And publication is a critical motivator and performance metric for the academic seeking tenure at any private or public institution' (McFadden, 2014). McFadden is right, of course, about how the 'machine of the academy' works. Academics are compelled to publish in peer-reviewed scholarly journals (and/or publish books with academic presses) in order to get hired and promoted. We will have more to say about metrics later (in Chapter Six), but for now we want to focus on the way the academy trains scholars, and here, Kristof is a bit closer to the mark.

'A basic challenge is that PhD programs have fostered a culture that glorifies arcane unintelligibility while disdaining impact and audience', Kristof charges about graduate training. The disdain for 'impact and audience' is certainly not the explicit goal of graduate programs, but rather an unintended consequence of them. The path to becoming a PhD is a long and arduous one (Bowen and Rudenstine, 1992), which takes an average of seven-and-a-half years to complete (Hoffer et al, 2006). The focus in designing PhD programs is producing new scholars who can do the work of a professional in their field. While there are wide variations across disciplines and institutions, few programs build a discussion about 'impact and audience' into their curricula for the PhD. The shift to digital scholarship implicitly raises these issues because of the openness and ease of measuring reach built into many tools.

Doctoral training at our institution, the Graduate Center at the City University of New York (CUNY), is somewhat unique in that there are several programs that emphasize the use of digital technology in research and in teaching. For example, the Interactive Technology and Pedagogy program offers courses in the use of technology in the classroom, leading to an additional certificate for graduate students.[1] The New Media Lab supports graduate students who are using digital media technologies in their doctoral research.[2] Through this lab, the provost's office has supported awards to students with 'digital dissertations' or dissertations that include a digital component. The CUNY Digital Humanities Initiative provides ongoing programming, workshops, and events designed by and for graduate students,[3] where faculty are welcome but not the target audience. Scores of graduate students with skills in digital media technologies have participated in the Macaulay Instructional Technology Fellowship program, where they work closely with faculty to incorporate technology into CUNY classrooms.[4] It is this kind of training in digital media technologies that contributes to a shift in academic culture, away from a legacy culture that 'glorifies arcane unintelligibility', while opening up scholarship to wider publics. We are fortunate to have so many opportunities for combining digital media technologies with graduate training, and these programs offer a model for other institutions. Without these programs and their collective contributions to the institutional infrastructure, our project would not have been possible. This type of training is still fairly unusual in graduate education, at least in the US, but it is impossible to chart precisely how rare, or prevalent, such programs might be.

There are no data, as far as we know, on the number or percentage of doctoral training programs that have digital technology offerings in their curricula. For the most part, the training that students in PhD programs receive in digital media technologies has been sporadic and inconsistent (Brescia and Miller, 2007, p. 180). If you are a graduate student who wants to learn about using digital technologies in your PhD research, at most institutions, there may be little training available. Without such training, graduate students are left to master these skills on their own, while completing an already arduous PhD program in their field.

Scholars who are well beyond the PhD and comfortably in mid-to-late career and want to learn to use digital technologies or craft a message about their research for a general audience have a handful of options. For instance, Anne Trubek, a former academic turned freelance writer and editor, offers online workshops specifically for faculty who want to learn how to pitch and submit pieces to editors at magazines and news organizations.[5] While not designed specifically for academics, The *OpEd Project*[6] offers workshops designed to increase the number of women who contribute commentary to mainstream news outlets. Both the *OpEd Project* and Trubek's workshops charge fees to participants, which for most academics is an out-of-pocket expense and non-reimbursable by their institution. The online platform *The Conversation*[7] is a collaboration between editors and academics that is designed to curate news analysis and commentary for a general audience and that is also free to read and republish. Begun in Australia, *The Conversation* now has continent- and country-specific versions in Africa, France, the UK, and the US. The backend of the platform uses a content management system (Ruby on Rails) with built-in features designed to help academics trained in specialized language of their discipline write for a broader audience. While learning through the interface is an important innovation, there is no other training for the scholar who wants to write for a general audience at *The Conversation*. For the scholar who wants to take up digital technologies in order to personally reach an audience beyond the academy, training is difficult to come by (Stein and Daniels, 2017).

For Kristof, this is bewildering because '[p]rofessors today have a growing number of tools available to educate the public, from online courses to blogs to social media' (Kristof, 2014b). He implores scholars to use these technologies in order to contribute to the 'great debates' about important social issues (Kristof, 2014b). There is a tension in Kristof's piece between the cloistered scholars publishing in obscure journals and those with tools – from online courses to blogs to social media – available to reach the public that hints at the uneven transition from legacy (focused only toward other scholars) to digital models of scholarship (more outward facing), which we discussed in Chapter Two. Tied to this, and part of the problem that Kristof identifies, is the legacy model of scholarly publishing, which is not geared toward openness (see Chapter Four). But even the ready and willing professors who might want to begin a transition to using digital media tools to reach a wide public audience, or simply learn to craft their research into messages for radio or television interviews, find little help from their own institutions or elsewhere whenever they look for training. Most scholars who begin using digital media technologies are self-taught.

The potential for a wide reach

'… I started the blog in 2007 as a teaching resource for myself and a handful of my friends', says Lisa Wade, a scholar and blogger. Almost a decade later, *Sociological Images*, Wade's blog, garners more than 20,000 readers every day (Wade and Sharp, 2013). Although she initially assumed that the blog's readers would be others in her field, Wade now reaches a broad, public audience with key insights from sociological research through compelling images. Today, a large percentage of her regular readers, about 80%, she estimates, are not involved in sociology at all, but are general readers (Stein and Daniels, 2017). Wade has extended the reach of her blog through social media like Facebook and Twitter. 'I try to make sure all of my Facebook and Twitter posts encapsulate an idea in themselves so that if … even if a person doesn't go to the blog, they still are getting a sociological lesson', she says. While the typical scholarly monograph may reach 100 or 200 people, and most journal articles even fewer, Wade reaches tens of thousands, sometimes hundreds of thousands, with a single post to social media. 'I would say that my typical Facebook post reaches 30,000 people. Most of them don't click, but that's still 30,000 people that saw an important sociological idea.' As a scholar, Wade says, 'It's a really interesting environment to be in' (Wade, 2015). Wade recently won an award for her blog from her professional association, and her success in building an audience for her blog also led to a book contract with a trade press (Stein and Daniels, 2017). But not every scholar may want to follow the innovative path that Wade has charted for herself.

What about the scholar who is not interested in reaching a wide audience – why should they bother with training in digital media technologies? The shortest, simplest answer to the question 'Why should I bother?' is: 'You don't have to'. Really, you don't have to be on television if CNN calls. You don't need a Twitter account. Scholars, including those early in their career, are successful academics without using digital media technologies. There are plenty of reasons to argue against the use of these technologies if you want to look for them (although, if you are reading this book, chances are you are looking for reasons to use digital technologies). Some of the most common arguments against engagement embrace the assumption that social media is a waste of time, that it dumbs down research, and that it is a distraction from more meaningful things such as publishing in peer-reviewed journals (Anselmo, 2015). The counter to these arguments exceed the parameters of this book, but scholars who are engaging in the world of ideas through digital media do not find it a waste of time (Stein and Daniels, 2017). Rather, public engagement through digital technology is an important extension of their academic work. There are many reasons why a scholar might *want* to engage with an array of technologies given the changes coming to the academy (Daniels and Feagin, 2011). As we described earlier (Chapter Two), digital media technologies are changing the structure of the habits of being a scholar.

Scholars might want to pursue training in digital media technologies in order to be recognized as an expert in a particular area, to build relationships, to engage with others to conceptualize and develop ideas, and to have an impact beyond a small circle of other experts.

But for scholars who want to reach a wide public audience through digital media technologies and don't know how to use these tools, there are few options available in the way of training that is tailored specifically to academics. Although academia is changing, opportunities for training in the hybrid skills of digital media technologies are still missing at most institutions. To us it seemed imperative to build this kind of training into our project.

Our experiment: MediaCamp workshops

'One month after the MediaCamp workshop, the President of Venezuela, Hugo Chavez, died of cancer, and all of a sudden I was besieged by media requests', says Sujatha Fernandes, a scholar who studies the popular culture of Latin America. 'That's really where the workshops came in very handy ... that's really what helped me feel comfortable and confident in the interviews' (Toral, 2014). Fernandes appeared on several cable news shows in the weeks that followed, but she says that none of her PhD training prepared her for this. 'We're taught to teach, we're taught to research, we're taught to write, but we're not usually taught how to talk to the media', says Fernandes (Toral, 2014). It was this gap in her training to be a scholar in the digital era that led Fernandes to attend several MediaCamp workshops.

MediaCamp, a series of workshops designed for academics and led by journalists, was a crucial component in our experiment with reimagining being a scholar in the digital era. MediaCamp was designed to address the general lack of training for faculty and graduate students in media training, both digital media technologies and more traditional media such as appearing on television or writing op-eds. It was also designed to intervene in a widely held belief we had observed among senior faculty that digital media technology was something for graduate students, but not something they could learn. This training in hybrid skills of journalism and digital media technologies was designed to sharpen academics' media skills through high-quality, hands-on, peer-to-peer instruction.

MediaCamp was designed for faculty and graduate students, but open to anyone who wanted to attend. Each workshop usually included a mix of participants, including faculty, graduate students, academic administrative assistants, non–governmental organization (NGO) workers, and community activists. All the workshops were offered at the CUNY Graduate School of Journalism and, thanks to grant funding from the Ford Foundation, were offered free of charge. The workshops were usually structured as three-hour sessions, with some didactic presentation and then lots of hands-on practice.

During its first year, MediaCamp featured more than 40 sessions, most with 10 to 20 participants (some with more), covering a range of topics including television interview techniques, writing for a general audience, creating a podcast, blogging, using Twitter, and making sense of web analytics. We repeated offerings of all these workshops several times during the calendar year, and we tested the interest in several other workshops, including ones about how to use smart phones in research, data visualization, digital media for research, communication strategy for social justice advocates, and creating image-driven presentations. It was this later set of workshops that were most popular with scholars who wanted training in these hybrid skills.

Being interviewed on camera

Being interviewed on camera is part of being a scholar in the digital era, as Sujatha Fernandes discovered. She received the on-camera MediaCamp training just prior to her MSNBC television appearance mentioned earlier in this chapter. Video shot by broadcast networks goes, almost immediately, to the web and then has a kind of digital permanence (Armstrong, 2006). The *Being Interviewed on Camera* workshop prepared academics to craft a message about their research in succinct, understandable language. Two veteran journalists with on-camera experience partnered to lead the workshop. Susan Farkas, a broadcast executive and journalist with experience at the Canadian Broadcasting Corporation (CBC), NBC News, and the United Nations, teamed with Fred Kaufman, a professor of English and journalism at the College of Staten Island, CUNY and a contributing editor for *Harper's* magazine who has a good deal of experience being on camera himself.

Before each workshop, participants were asked to prepare a short statement about their research. Then, organizers solicited volunteers to sit for mock television interviews, with Kaufman role-playing as the worst kind of aggressive interviewer. During the workshop, instructors and participants reviewed the video of the mock interviews recorded earlier in the same day. For the remainder of the workshop, Farkas and Kaufman shared guidelines for on-camera behavior, staying on message, pivoting back to the message when the interviewer tried to steer the conversation in an unexpected direction, and emphasizing the importance of appearing confident. Farkas and Kaufman encouraged participants to 'own' an interview by adjusting and reapplying what they already did well in a college classroom. The on camera workshop was the most expensive workshop to produce, due to the costs of equipment rental and studio time. The practical experience, reassurance, and direction the workshop offered also made it one of the most worthwhile, even for seasoned academic speakers.

The feedback we received about the on camera workshops was mostly very positive and enthusiastic. One participant said: 'What I loved about this session was the way the instructors used the participants' own materials as the basis of the discussion'. Another found the workshop provided 'concrete professional guidance that I would not have had access to otherwise'. One participant enthused: 'Great initiative – there is such a huge need for workshops like these' (JustPublics@365, 2014). In general, these fervent responses confirmed our hunch that there was a tremendous unmet need for this kind of training. We also heard negative reactions about this workshop and especially from women academics, including some who had not even taken the workshop. One woman said, 'Oh, I would never sign up for such a workshop – I am not made for TV!' Another woman, who did take the workshop, said afterwards: 'Well they [the instructors] were great but it was just so hard to see myself on camera – I am not ready for TV'.

The reticence we heard almost always from women is, at least in part, about the fact that women are still judged more harshly based on their appearance. This cultural phenomenon gets internalized and heightened through being on camera. It affects whose voices are heard in the public sphere. Some have pointed to the women's own harsh self-criticism about their appearance on camera as a reason that there are fewer women featured as pundits (Wente, 2014), while others point to supply-side issues with who gets called on for television talk shows (Mundy, 2014). Overall, *Being Interviewed on Camera* offered a useful set of skills for scholars like Sujatha Fernandes, who shortly after her session was appearing on a cable news show talking about her work.

Op-Ed Pitches & Pieces: framing research for public audiences

'There is nothing important that cannot be made interesting', notes journalist Ezra Klein (Blattman, 2015). In many ways, the *Op-Ed Pitches & Pieces* workshop was meant to help academics craft their research into interesting prose for a general reader. Deborah Stead, a journalist for 25 years, an editor at the *New York Times*, *BusinessWeek*, and *Oxygen Media*, led most of these workshops, where her first focus was on helping academics to recognize a 'news peg' for an op-ed or article. The 'news peg' – what makes the story timely or newsworthy right now – is basic for journalists but can seem mystifying for academics. For example, for research about the history of voting rights, the news peg might be a recent election. Understanding how to connect academic research, which may be conducted over many years, to a much shorter news cycle is one of the challenges that scholars face when trying to place their work into a broader conversation in the public sphere.

In each workshop, Stead asked a working editor at a major news outlet to join the workshop for a question and answer session with participants. Stead's long history of working with major news organizations, and the location of the CUNY Graduate School of Journalism next door to the *New York Times* building, made this possible. Stead used these conversations to guide participants through the process of pitching to a news outlet and, should the piece be accepted, working with a news editor on that piece. This process can be daunting, as it is very different from the one that scholars go through with an editor of an academic journal.

Op-Ed Pitches & Pieces was one of the larger workshops we offered, with attendance that was often close to 30 participants. The professional background of the participants varied and included graduate students, professors at all ranks, and people who identified as working in non-profits or NGOs. The responses from participants were universally glowing, without any of the reservations expressed about the *Being Interviewed on Camera* workshop.

Podcasting

'We're in a golden age of podcasting', observed Kevin Roose (2014). The migration of long-form audio storytelling from radio to digital and downloadable formats began with the introduction of the iPod in 2001 (hence, the name 'podcasting'). Even though the device has been discontinued, the name has lingered and the genre of podcasts has become very popular since 2009 or so. Some 46 million people in the US listened to at least one podcast per month, according to one media analysis (Edison Research, 2015).

One of the best of these is *Invisibilia,* which takes academic research and enlivens it through sophisticated storytelling, like the episode about the man who is blind but navigates his way around using echolocation. This form appeals to our 'love of storytelling and neuroscience' (Larson, 2015). It also appeals to academics who want to reach wider audiences, and it is why we offered a workshop in podcasting.

Our podcasting workshops were led by Heidi Knoblauch, a self-taught podcast producer and then a PhD student in medical history. The workshops offered participants both some ideas about the strategies behind podcast development and then hands-on practice in how to create a podcast using Garageband (application software that is standard on all Mac computers). During the workshop, participants used smartphones to record audio. Then, they imported it into their computers and did some basic editing in Garageband. At the end, Knoblauch took participants through the steps required to publish their completed work to iTunes. The feedback we received on these workshops was generally positive but the consensus among participants, even those with some existing digital skills, was that this was a lot to learn in one three-hour session.

Twitter for academics

'There were 3 million tweets about Ferguson before mass media outlets picked it up', said Zeynep Tufekci, a scholar at the School of Information and Library Science at the University of North Carolina, at the October 2015 Ithaka Conference held in New York City.[8] When her Twitter feed filled August 9, 2014 with tweets about the Ferguson, Missouri police killing of Michael Brown and the protests it immediately prompted, Tufekci shifted, at some point, to Facebook. Instead of finding updates about the police action and protests in Ferguson, her Facebook feed continued to be lined with posts about the ice bucket challenge (this stunt to encourage donations for research on ALS, or motor neurone disease as it is known in the UK, was ubiquitously shared on social media, peaking in July–August 2014).

Tufekci cites Facebook's 'tendency toward the positive, toward the "like"' (there was, at the time, no Facebook 'dislike') as a quality that might not lend the platform to social movement communication and critical analysis in the way that Twitter does. Social media platforms are not created alike, and in this case not curated alike, with Facebook's algorithms suppressing news items in Tufekci's feed that her friends were posting about Ferguson (Tufekci, 2015). But at this time at least, the Twitter hashtag allows users to target access to conversation to a greater degree. Communities assemble themselves on social media platforms for different social and political purposes. Twitter is the platform of choice for social movement activism and, perhaps not coincidently, for academic exchange.

Our MediaCamp workshop on Twitter was led by Sandeep Junnarkar, an associate professor at the CUNY Graduate School of Journalism and director of the Interactive Journalism Program. Junnarkar's pre-academic professional credits include leadership as the breaking news editor, writer, and web producer when *The New York Times on the Web* went live. Junnarkar began Twitter workshops with a conceptual discussion about why academics might want to bother with Twitter. He emphasized the platform's conversational quality and usefulness to academics for building relationships over its use as a tool to simply broadcast posts about academic work. In the workshop, Junnarkar walked participants through how to set up a profile and then took them through some of the nuances of the platform's particular jargon and capabilities, such as the difference between @ replies and direct messages, how to retweet, create lists, and 'tune' one's Twitter timeline for 'more signal and less noise'.

Blogging

From afar, the success that Lisa Wade has had with her blog *Sociological Images* could seem easy. But launching and maintaining a scholarly blog can be a daunting task. Under the expert guidance, once again, of Sandeep Junnarkar, we offered a series of blogging workshops that introduced scholars to the benefits of blogging, or engaging in non-academic writing for academic and non-academic publics.

Junnarkar guided attendees through the process of establishing a blog, discussed the merits of several free plug-and-play blogging platforms, and then delved more deeply into WordPress.com. He reviewed the nuts and bolts of writing a post, title, and excerpt for each entry, uploading and/or embedding media (photographs and pdfs), hyperlinking to other work, changing design themes, and updating already published posts.

Participants completed the workshop with a branded, personal site on the WordPress platform, and the knowledge that other platforms such as Tumblr, Weebly, and Wix provide reasonable alternatives. WordPress's extensive assembly of settings and plugins allow easy embedding for video, photos, and audio to expand the blogs' interest and narrative richness. Participants left the workshop with links to Junnarkar's instruction notes. Later, attendees benefited from a *Toolkit*, a pdf eBook that summarized the content of all nine social media workshops (JustPublics@365, 2013b). The blogging workshop tied thematically to the workshops on op-ed writing, by sharing a focus on writing crisply and compellingly – or storytelling – for non-academic audiences.

Analytics and metrics

What good is a blog or a Tweet if nobody reads it, and how do you know when they do? In the *Analytics and Metrics* workshops, Junnarkar explored how Google can be applied to track website traffic. With an eye on site analytics, bloggers can tweak publication schedules, attract readers with well-designed metadata (appropriately chosen keywords), and adapt content to increase discovery and to draw more online visitors who review more content. Twitter analytics, too, are useful to keep an eye on, to better understand when tweets are read the most, by whom, and with what result.

We envisioned these three workshops – Twitter, blogging, and analytics – as something of a set curriculum. They were designed to introduce academics to social media basics (Twitter), to the increasingly more involved (blogging), and even the advanced and complex (analytics and metrics) elements of social media work, though most attendees did not take the workshops in this sequenced path.

What we learned from training scholars for the digital era

Our experiment with training scholars for the digital era met with both resistance and enthusiasm. When launching MediaCamp, we explained the concept to one senior faculty member, who folded his arms and said, 'I will not be made to learn the internet! I will retire before that happens.' Another equally accomplished scholar at the same institution had a very different response. She signed up for nearly all the digital media workshops, and explained her motivation this way: 'I have younger scholars who come to me and want to collaborate with tools I don't understand, so I want to be able to work with them'. There were a range of other responses between these two opposing reactions, but among the participants we surveyed, most reported that MediaCamp helped them become more engaged scholars, like Sujatha Fernandes, who was able to confidently respond to media requests after her sessions (JustPublics@365, 2014a).

In general, we found that learning digital media skills could be both intimidating and exhilarating for faculty. Professors often 'fear the awkwardness of relearning their profession' (Shor and Freire, 2003, p. 479). For scholars who long ago established themselves as experts in their fields, the idea of beginning to learn a fresh set of skills can be intimidating or even demeaning (Shor and Freire, 2003, p. 479). While some scholars feel a painful loss of status when they are not the expert, others responded differently. Some scholars relish the prospect being a beginner, of diving into unknown worlds and the playfulness of handling a new tool. We found it impossible to predict these different affective responses as they emerged from scholars across every discipline and a range of institutions.

We found that the 'guide at the side' pedagogy works best for training scholars in the digital era (King, 1993). The format of each workshop included an instructor and an assistant working with a small group of participants, each at a lab computer or on their own laptop. As each participant followed the instructor's direction, the assistant, and sometimes the instructor, could offer hands-on help when needed. For some participants who were totally new to a digital environment, the learning curve could be steep. Several of our participants took the same workshop several times. Many more scholars wanted to attend workshops, or take them again, but they could not due to their primary work commitments to research and teaching. The January break between semesters proved to be the most popular time for workshops, as teaching commitments were often reduced. Summer was somewhat popular, but not as much as we had hoped. The myth is that faculty have 'summers off', but in fact, the summer months are when faculty who both teach and do research finish many of their writing projects. Academics guard this time very closely. In addition, professors with young children often have increased childcare responsibilities when their children's schools are out for summer. Scheduling at most other times during the long semester was more art than science as we struggled to find times that worked for most faculty and graduate students who juggled many commitments.

With the high demand and difficulty with scheduling in-person sessions, we explored the idea of offering online versions of the workshops. However, what we found was similar to the lessons learned about the commercial MOOCs (massive open online courses – see Chapter Three). Recorded lectures work best for those who already have a leg up on the material, but they do not work as well for those who need a 'guide at the side'. What our experiment taught us is that it is difficult to train scholars for the digital era in massive numbers. In digital terms, 'it does not scale'.

We learned, too, from the generation of scholars who are just beginning their careers, about their concerns regarding the use of digital media technologies. For this younger generation of scholars, the Internet has been part of their lives for as long as they can remember. They are fluent in many digital technologies and they seem to quickly and effortlessly learn new ones. But, like more senior scholars, many early career scholars also struggle to craft the central idea of their research into language that general audiences understand. The deeper concerns about digital technologies are tied to the austerity politics in which they emerge. For instance, Karen Gregory is troubled by the additional labor that digital media requires of faculty at a time when an increasing majority are precariously employed, especially when that labor is publicly performed (Gregory, 2013). Mark Carrigan is alarmed by the acceleration of academic life that he witnesses. He worries that we are losing the benefits of a slower, more contemplative pace that is necessary for cultivating sustained critiques and complex arguments (Carrigan, 2016a). Tressie McMillan Cottom urges that we attend to social inequities, historical and contemporary racism and sexism that makes some scholars more vulnerable than others in forms of knowledge production that traffic in digital attention economies (Cottom, 2015). In conversation with these concerns and many different affective responses from faculty, the MediaCamp workshops addressed unmet needs among both established and emerging scholars for training in digital media technologies.

Community activists, non-profit and NGO staffers also participated in MediaCamp workshops and this did several things. It gave them training they needed and were not getting elsewhere. We learned from participants in the workshops that because they were younger, their supervisors often assumed they 'knew about the Internet', so they assigned them the task of running the social media accounts for their organization. Many expressed dismay at this assignment, since they were unfamiliar with digital media beyond their own personal use. Participation by community activists in MediaCamp also fostered and strengthened collaborations with academics; among the participants were members of the East Harlem community who had participated in the #InQ13 course. Offering MediaCamp, geared to academics but open to all, positioned CUNY as a reliable resource for this kind of training in the city and the region.

An unintended consequence of our MediaCamp workshops was to highlight the unclear relationship between academic institutions and digital media technologies. Low-paid administrative university staff were regular attendees. These staffers, like many non-profit and NGO workers who attended, signed up for the workshops because they had been assigned the task of administering the social media accounts for their departments, centers, or schools. Yet, they had not generally received training or guidelines about how to use these technologies. They were also usually not being paid extra to take on additional responsibilities. Colleges and universities must develop significant administrative communications infrastructures, including staff hiring and training, to employ digital media technologies effectively. Compensation for additional responsibilities should be of interest to labor unions. The staffers we met were not working with their university publicity officers who, their impression was, were generally not focused on their efforts with social media. Departmental and chief administrators were mostly inattentive to staff efforts with social media. While some may think the use of social media for institutional purposes is 'free' or low cost, it actually has significant staffing and training costs. In this way, MediaCamp helped to support our own institution's (and other institutions') communication infrastructure needs.

While some fear that scholars will someday be required to use digital media, we did not see evidence of this among the faculty and graduate students who attended the workshops (Carrigan, 2016a). While it was often the case that managing digital media had become a job requirement for non-profit workers and academic administrative assistants, it was not true for faculty or graduate students. The academics, both early career and more senior, who attended our workshops, expressed a strong interest in learning skills that would help them reach a wider audience. This emerging practice of scholars actively creating their own media content through multiple channels to represent themselves and share their work, however, presents a new set of challenges for colleges and universities.

The rising scholarly use of digital media technologies means that faculty are often working as their own press agents and circumventing the gatekeeping and assistance of their university's press office. One way to view faculty engagement through media – digital and otherwise – is that this labor benefits a college or university. To the extent that an individual faculty member links their online presence to their institution, every bit of their effort to circulate ideas links to their institution as well. To date, there has been a wide array of institutional responses to faculty engagement, generally ranging from faint praise to laissez-faire concern, to harsh retaliation, and even to termination (Flaherty, 2015; Stein and Daniels, 2017). When scholars come under attack for what they say through social media, from individuals, from institutions, or from individuals who want to force institutions to rescind job offers, this raises new questions about being a scholar in the digital era. We did not include a MediaCamp workshop on how to manage backlash, but future iterations would do well to include a session that offers guidance about what to do if attacked and how to be supportive of public scholars (Grollman, 2015). University press offices are smart to reimagine their work when scholars increasingly act as their own press agents. College and university presidents, provosts, and boards should carefully consider policies for the digital era that support faculty engagement and protect academic freedom.

MediaCamp: critical information literacy for scholars in the digital era

From a library and information science perspective, MediaCamp is a form of 'information literacy' or 'media literacy' training. Traditional information literacy competency standards, adopted by academic library organizations around the world, have come under sharp criticism from librarians who view them as a tool applied to shape student learning in a manner that does not ultimately serve student interests.

Critics contend that information literacy standards assume that research and analysis are procedural and predominantly neutral (Seale, 2010, p. 222). Such standards reify hierarchies of knowledge production and consumption. When information literacy teaches generic research skills, it reinforces the management and measurement systems of neoliberal institutions (Accardi et al, 2010; Drabinski, 2014). Librarians critical of this approach have made good use of Twitter to raise awareness about their critique of information literacy standards and practices. The #critlib hashtag is popularly used to signal conversation about a shift away from instruction to accomplish positivist 'outcomes' of performance and toward attention to the politics, power, and industry of knowledge production.

MediaCamp does not fit a standard information literacy agenda. Designed for the local, immediate needs of faculty and graduate students, MediaCamp shifts information literacy instruction from a standard-based concern to modes of digital production and engagement with non-academic publics. MediaCamp embraces media literacy goals, supplementing scholars' training in traditional formats with training in the production and use of audio, visual, and social media. The workshops put scholars in dialogue with media and journalism professionals about the mechanisms of media production, and offered training and skills about how to work with the popular press and social media.

One of the latent goals of MediaCamp was to raise the perceived value of interacting with the public for scholars. This kind of training enables scholars to interact publicly, to build professional reputations, to effect change, and to participate in broader arenas without the usual gatekeepers. Such training can equip scholars to become digitally fluent teachers, better able to guide students in a critical understanding of what it means to be a 'prosumer', both a producer and a consumer of knowledge in the digital era (Ritzer and Jurgenson, 2010).

Forward thinking: training to be relevant

Being a scholar in the digital era means being concerned with the world beyond the academy and openly engaging with it. Kristof's damning assessment with which this chapter began – 'to be a scholar is, often, to be irrelevant' (Kristof, 2014b) – is half true but speaks to a legacy model of scholarship geared toward a cloistered existence. For that to change, for scholars to become more engaged in and through digital media, they will have to be able to acquire those skills. Currently, there are very few options for scholars who want this kind of training.

Our experiment with MediaCamp at the Graduate Center, CUNY, was designed to offer such training through intra-institutional collaboration between the main PhD-granting arm of the university, the Graduate School of Journalism, and the Graduate Center's research library. The MediaCamp collaboration was successful for the institution, and it also fostered many scholars at our institution and throughout the region to be engaged with wider publics. MediaCamp provided a bridge between university and community partners, and the no-fee structure contributed to the mission of CUNY to not only train our faculty, but also to educate the 'children of the whole people' of New York.

Forward thinking academic institutions will soon realize that they have a vested interest in the use of digital media by faculty and staff. For administrative use of social media, colleges and universities must recognize that the expert use of digital media is a set of skills that takes time to acquire and should be fairly compensated. The people who lead colleges and universities should recognize that each time a scholar invests time in engaging beyond the academy while flying the flag of their institution, they are contributing to the collective good of the institution, to the community it serves, and to the larger public good.

More broadly, having scholars more engaged in the public sphere is crucial for a vibrant democracy. Colleges and universities can be vibrant contributors to a collective intellectual life and to material progress on our most pressing social, civic, economic, and moral problems, but to do this, scholars across disciplines and institutions must become more engaged (Boyer, 1996, p. 18). Digital media technologies provide a tremendous opportunity for the scholarship of engagement. Innovative colleges and universities will find ways to either offer training in digital media technologies directly, as we did, or support it indirectly through reimbursement for continuing education costs.

The need for training will not be solved by generational turnover in the faculty. The pressing issues of today will not wait for a new generation. Given the shrinking pool of tenured or tenurable faculty in permanent positions, and the growing number of adjunct faculty in temporary positions, a generational turnover may happen, but it will be a long time coming. Precariously employed faculty are also engaged scholar-activists, and forward-thinking institutions will find ways to address their concerns or risk damage to their brand, and more seriously to their service to the community. Finally, this problem will not solve itself without intervention. Even faculty who have grown up with the Internet often do not know how to use it in scholarly work. The need for training in digital media technologies in colleges and universities persists even as younger scholars join the academy.

Scholarly societies and associations, too, have a vested interest in their members becoming engaged scholars. When Annette Lareau became president of the American Sociological Association (ASA) in 2014, she wanted to use her time as the leader of this important scholarly society to get sociologists more engaged beyond the academy, as Lisa Wade has done through her blog, *Sociological Images*. In her year as president, Lareau developed multiple strategies for achieving her goal, including the formation of a Task Force for Engaged Sociologists. As part of the task force, Lareau invited our MediaCamp to the annual meeting of the association to help train scholars in digital media technologies and in crafting their research for sharing with a wide public audience. There, we held a day-long pre-conference series of workshops that closely followed the models we had implemented at our own institution. What Lareau recognized is that the ASA as a whole would benefit if more scholars talked about their work to wider publics. Forward-thinking scholarly societies and associations may follow Lareau's lead and begin to view training in digital media technologies as a benefit they could provide for members in exchange for association dues and conference fees.

Engagement with a wider public is not rewarded in the academy, for the most part. It is not, as Syreeta McFadden put it in her critique of Kristof's remarks, 'how the machine of the academy works' (McFadden, 2014). That machine relies on publication in peer-reviewed journals and scholarly monographs as the primary metrics for assessing academic performance. It is to metrics that we turn next. These, too, are changing in the digital era.

Notes

1. See www.gc.cuny.edu/Page-Elements/Academics-Research-Centers-Initiatives/Certificate-Programs/Interactive-Technology-and-Pedagogy
2. See http://newmedialab.cuny.edu/
3. See http://cunydhi.commons.gc.cuny.edu/
4. See http://macaulay.cuny.edu/eportfolios/itfprogram/
5. See https://thethinkingwriter.wordpress.com/how-to-pitch-submit/
6. See www.theopedproject.org
7. See www.theconversation.com
8. See www.ithaka.org/conference

SIX

Measuring scholarly impact

> I do a lot of work with colleges and universities, and study countless catalogs, and it won't surprise you to hear that almost every college catalog in this country still lists teaching, research, and service as the priorities of the professoriate. (Boyer, 1996, p. 22)

In the last speech of his life, Ernest Boyer, then president of the Carnegie Foundation for the Advancement of Teaching, explained the landscape of measuring scholarly impact. He also wanted to change it. Boyer wanted to expand the way academics think about the third leg of the three-legged table of scholarly impact: 'It won't surprise you either that at tenure and promotion time, the harsh truth is that service is hardly mentioned.' Even more disturbing to Boyer was the penalty against faculty who did that kind of work. He observed that researchers who spent time on 'so-called applied projects frequently jeopardize their careers' (Boyer, 1996, p. 22). Speaking in October 1995 on the cusp of the emerging popular Internet, Boyer issued a loud and clear call for a less insular university and for academics to become 'more vigorously engaged in the issues of our day' (Boyer, 1996, p. 28). He would not live to see the rise of networked scholarship – Boyer died just two months after he gave that speech – but in many ways being a scholar in the digital era realizes much of what he envisioned.

Bonnie Stewart, in her recent analysis of how Boyer's vision of scholarship is playing out in the digital era, finds that the networked engagement of digital scholars fulfills what he imagined and takes it even further (Stewart, 2015). Boyer said there was a need to recognize, and value, different kinds of scholarship. Boyer wanted college and university faculty to become 'vigorously engaged with the issues of our day' but there would need to be some way to recognize and value different kinds of scholarly work, which he called the 'scholarship of engagement' (Boyer, 1990). Under the broad category of the 'scholarship of engagement,' Boyer enumerates five types of scholarship: (1) discovering knowledge, (2) integrating knowledge, (3) sharing of knowledge, (4) the application of knowledge, and (5) teaching (Boyer, 1990). In her perceptive analysis, Stewart uses Twitter updates from academics to illustrate each of Boyer's five types of scholarship. Stewart's work suggests that digitally networked scholarship embodies Boyer's initial aim of broadening scholarship itself through fostering extensive cross-disciplinary, public ties and rewarding connection, collaboration, and curation between individual scholars, rather than through their institutions or professional roles. Stewart's point is clear: the scholarship of engagement has arrived.

Digital technologies have transformed the infrastructure of participation in scholarship in ways that Boyer might never have imagined. The academically focused search engine Google Scholar uses algorithms to search the text of millions of peer-reviewed journal articles, including those behind publishers' paywalls. A majority of scholars now use it. A recent survey among scientists found that roughly 60% use Google Scholar regularly (van Noorden, 2014).

Anurag Acharya, who co-created and still runs Google Scholar, is an example of someone who is doing the scholarship of engagement that Boyer called for, both applying his knowledge of algorithms to the vast body of academic literature and making it more widely available. Acharya's work is also having an impact. He recalls:

> I came to Google in 2000, as a year off from my academic job at the University of California, Santa Barbara. It was pretty clear that I was unlikely to have a larger impact [in academia] than at Google – making it possible for people everywhere to be able to find information. (van Noorden, 2014)

The other people working on Google Scholar are 'all, in part, ex-academics', Acharya explains. He and his colleagues collaborate on one of the digital technologies that are changing the infrastructure of being a scholar. Part of the larger and profitable Internet giant Google, the smaller Scholar operation does not make money. 'The primary role of Scholar is to give back to the research community, and we are able to do so because it is not very expensive, from Google's point of view', explains Acharya (van Noorden, 2014). In supporting the non-revenue-generating Scholar, Google is playing a role that foundations and universities once played in creating non-for-profit presses.

To be absolutely clear, the non–profit Scholar is made possible precisely because it exists within the larger and very profitable Google, which is essentially a digital media advertising company (Vaidhyanathan, 2011). This should concern scholars for a variety of reasons, including the surveillance and threats to privacy, and the constant threat that services we come to rely on when they are offered at no cost will suddenly only be available for a premium monthly charge (Vaidhyanathan, 2011). Despite these concerns, a survey found that a majority of scholars now use this search service and find it beneficial for their work (van Noorden, 2014).

'The benefits that Scholar provides ,,, are very significant', Acharya contends (van Noorden, 2014). But how would those 'very significant benefits' be evaluated in the academy? If Acharya had stayed in his academic position and developed the same innovative search platform there, how would his university measure the impact of his work? It is impossible to know for sure, but in all likelihood Acharya would have been discouraged from working on such a large, collaborative and applied project until after tenure. If he had disregarded such advice and continued working on it, he could have ended up as one of the cases Boyer mentioned of scholars who are punished for doing applied scholarship.

Anurag Acharya's career and contribution to being a scholar in the digital era raises questions about how measuring scholarly impact is changing. Most of the attention to the 'priorities of the professoriate' – teaching, research and service, as Boyer named them – is on scholarship, and on quantitative measures of impact. To appreciate both Boyer's call for the scholarship of engagement and Acharya's contribution to the transformations in being a scholar, it is important to understand the influence of Eugene Garfield on the whole ecosystem of measuring scholarly impact.

The (unintended) impact of Eugene Garfield on academia

'Is there anything comparable to your impact worldwide?', an interviewer asked Eugene Garfield, comparing his influence to that of Sputnik on space technology (Hargittai, 1999, p. 26). Garfield deflected the interviewer's comparison as hyperbole, but then wondered on his own, 'I can't imagine how you would evaluate the impact of my work.

How would you measure it?' (Hargittai, 1999, p. 26). His rhetorical question is deeply ironic, given Garfield's outsized influence on how academics measure impact (Jasco, 2010).

If you dig very deep at all into how academics think about measuring scholarly impact today, you are bound to encounter the work of Eugene Garfield. A native of the Bronx, Garfield grew up in a Jewish and Italian household, where his early years were shaped by 'two uncles who were Marxists' and an absentee father who was a successful businessman (Small, 2007). Garfield would go on to become an influential figure, and a wealthy man, because of the information tools he created. His tools changed the way scholars are employed, professors at universities are given tenure, and research journals are judged for their quality (Hargittai, 1999, p. 26; Jasco, 2010). He created the *Science Citation Index* (SCI), the *Arts and Humanities Citation Index* (AHCI) and the *Social Sciences Citation Index* (SSCI) (Garfield, 1955). For scholars working today, the SCI and SSCI are the standard metrics for assessing scholarly impact of research published in peer-reviewed journals. Divided by disciplines, each index tracks the number of times an article is cited in other journals. Every scholar who has published an article in a peer-reviewed science or social science journal has an entry in the SCI or SSCI. Associated with each name is a count and an indexed list of the citations their work has garnered.

A hybrid scientist and information specialist, Garfield holds degrees in both chemistry and library science, and he earned a PhD in structural linguistics, with a dissertation project that combined chemistry and library science. Born in 1925, he developed his citation analysis in the 1950s. Retired now, but still active, Garfield founded the Institute for Scientific Information (ISI), a company that eventually became one of the world's largest commercial providers of scientific research data. Garfield is widely credited with founding the fields of bibliometrics (the statistical analysis of written publications) and scientometrics (the study of measuring and analyzing science, technology, and innovation). Garfield has also been called the 'grandfather of Google Scholar' for his innovative work on citation indexing, which laid the theoretical basis for the algorithm underneath the popular search platform (Bensman, 2013).

'Citation analysis exposed the political nature of East European science academies – many academicians were administrators, not world-class scientists', Garfield explained to an interviewer (Hargittai, 1999, p. 26). Garfield developed citation indexing as a way to spot scientific trends and to trace how an idea flows through the scholarly literature (Garfield, 1955). Garfield extended his work with citation analysis to the extent that he could predict Nobel laureates with a good degree of accuracy (Garfield and Malin, 1968). Disrupting the political nature of promotion in the academy was an unintended consequence of his citation analysis. 'In Italy, the SCI was like salvation to some scientists' for the way it could highlight the 'unfair allocation of credit and resources' (Hargittai, 1999, p. 26).

'If the SCI is used in tenure evaluations, hopefully it is done intelligently', Garfield explains (Hargittai, 1999, p. 26). Some institutions have been known to measure the length of the indexed citations in inches for an individual scholar's tenure case (Stein and Daniels, 2016): more inches (in citations), more impact. This runs counter to what Garfield has advocated throughout his career: that his 'automatic and objective' measures should be used in combination with peer evaluations (Garfield and Malin, 1968, p. 7). Still, academic institutions with a management mindset find the promise of 'automatic and objective' measures irresistible.

Building on the SCI and SSCI, Garfield also created the 'journal impact factor' (Garfield, 2005). The journal impact factor (JIF) figures prominently in the UK's measurement system for academic performance, the Research Excellence Framework (REF). The way it is used in most academic institutions, and the way it works in British universities, the JIF is regarded as a valid and reliable measure of scholarly impact. The JIF rates journals as a whole – not individual articles. To get this number, Garfield constructed a formula that analyzes the most recent one or two years of citations to articles in the journal (Garfield, 2006). As with many quantitative measures, such as a random-dial survey, the JIF provides a snapshot of a moment in time – in this case, the most recent two years. The JIF includes all citations to articles in a journal, including citations to articles published by the journal itself. This means that editors who want to raise their impact factor can do things to manipulate it, including publishing review articles that already include a large number of citations from that journal, both of which translate into a higher rating for the journal. It is common practice among journal editors, once an article is accepted for publication, to ask authors to add a few citations from that particular publication, known as 'coercive citations'. This practice is so commonplace, writes one professor of engineering, that scholars anticipate what is expected and 'load their articles with citations from the journal to which they are submitting before they are even asked' (Hoole, 2014).

While some regard the JIF as one of the highest standards of peer-review measures, critics contend that it is little more than a measure of popularity and takes a very short-term view of impact. Critics contend that this means that the JIF provides a misleading indication of the true impact of journals, biased in favor of journals that have a quick impact, as is the pattern in the sciences, rather than a prolonged impact, as happens more often in the social sciences and humanities (Vanclay, 2008). One analysis finds that the journal impact factor is 'bad scientific practice' as a way to measure scholarly impact (Brembs et al, 2013). This is not simply a critique of Garfield's tool, but rather their data suggest that 'any journal rank (not only the currently-favored Impact Factor) would have this negative impact'. Instead, they suggest abandoning journals altogether, in favor of a library-based scholarly communication system, which would use information technology to vastly improve the filter, sort and discovery functions of the current journal system (Brembs et al, 2013).

Some are so frustrated with the tool that Garfield created that they are taking action to have the JIF eliminated from any and all evaluation measures. In 2012, a group of scholars, journal editors and publishers, scholarly societies, and research funders across a range of disciplines issued a declaration calling on the world scientific community to stop using the JIF in evaluating research for funding, hiring, promotion, or institutional effectiveness (Stein and Daniels, 2016). To date, more than 12,500 individuals and 585 organizations have signed on to the San Francisco Declaration on Research Assessment (DORA).[1]

'When we talk about intellectual impact, it is very subjective', concedes Garfield, although the tools he invented are widely regarded as being objective measures of impact. Of course, the evaluation of scholarly impact is more complicated than simply assigning a number. The assessment of scholarly impact is a complex evaluative process (Lamont, 2009). The process assumes an elite circle of readers deemed knowledgeable enough to assess quality and excellence. The review process in decisions about tenure, promotion, and grant awards is a deliberative one, in which the terms 'quality' and 'excellence' are hotly contested in the process (Lamont, 2009; Lamont and Huutoniemi, 2011). How scholars evaluate each other's research varies, based on setting (internal review for hiring, tenure, and promotion), institution (elite research-focused universities or teaching-focused community colleges), and national context (Lamont, 2012). Quantitative indices, like the ones Garfield developed, are meant to serve as proxy measures for research quality and scholarly impact.

Garfield's tools and the impact agenda

There is an animated and nuanced discussion about how to measure scholarly impact in the UK, in large part because there is a funding structure for higher education there that relies heavily on the REF,[2] introduced in 2014. The REF emerged from a series of changes to higher education and other sectors in Britain, beginning in the early 1980s in the Thatcher years. Then began what many have now come to refer to as 'audit culture' and 'new managerialism', both expressions of a more global process of neoliberal economic and political transformation (Shore and Wright, 2003, p. 58).

With the Education Reform Act 1988, academics lost the security of tenure, and the funding of universities was tied to performance measures. Under royal charters, universities set their own standards and were the sole arbiters of their own quality. Audit culture, introduced by the Education Reform Act, marked a significant break with the principle of academic autonomy (Shore and Wright, 2003, p. 70). It laid the groundwork for the REF, and set current standards for judging scholarly impact in the UK.

The shift to audit culture in British higher education required departments to submit 'bids' claiming their provision to be 'excellent,' 'satisfactory' or 'unsatisfactory' (Shore and Wright, 2003, p. 70). Any university department deemed unsatisfactory had to rectify the situation within 12 months, or else 'core funding' would be withdrawn' (Shore and Wright, 2003, p. 70). The changing policies for higher education in the UK, writes John Holmwood, British sociologist and former head of the British Sociological Association, subordinates higher education to the market in ways that systematically undermine the idea of a public university and education for all (Holmwood, 2011). The rise in audit culture, and with it the push to measure impact, is part of the larger trend toward seeing higher education as a private commodity rather than a public good (Holmwood, 2011).

The meaning of 'teaching quality' has also been transformed by the audit culture of the neoliberal university. To be audited, the learning experience must now be quantified and standardized so that it can be measured. The curriculum's merits are today measured in terms of finite, tangible, transferable and, above all, marketable skills (Shore and Wright, 2003, pp. 72–3). If students are merely customers, then it becomes easier to shift the burden of paying for higher education onto them, while placing the burden of demonstrating 'satisfactory' impact onto faculty and a new army of academic administrators.

In the US, there is a fairly wide discussion within academia about scholarly engagement, prompted by Boyer's work, but compared to the UK, there is relatively little discussion beyond a few circles in the US about how to measure scholarly impact in bibliometrics or scientometrics, the areas of study that Garfield helped to launch. Rather than talk about an 'impact agenda', as is common in the UK, an analogous discussion in the US might be called the 'success agenda,' and it is usually framed by terms like 'teaching effectiveness', student 'outcomes' or the 'success' of students. The 'success agenda' in the US is led most vociferously by those advocating for charter schools, which are pre-college learning institutions that are also being transformed into corporate-style revenue generators (Fabricant and Fine, 2012). Those championing the success agenda in higher education in the US are those who pose questions such as: 'how well do graduates do a decade after their degrees? What do graduates [actually learn]?' (DeMillo, 2015, p. 17). Such questions are supposedly meant to promote measures of impact that are 'student-centered' rather than 'faculty-centered' (DeMillo, 2015). The suggestion to do away with research in universities is not truly one that serves the interests of students, who are often involved in and learn from research, but rather one that is economically centered but disguised as being student-centered.

There are no reliable comparative data on the use of metrics and methods of evaluations internationally (Lamont, 2012). For the two cases with which we are most familiar, the US and the UK, the underlying logic for the way 'impact' is understood is strikingly similar. Both the impact agenda in academia in the UK and the success agenda in the US are driven by the logic of the neoliberal marketplace. In the UK, the impact agenda is part of a broader audit culture and, in the US, the success agenda is part of the relentless focus on 'student outcomes' and 'achievement gaps.' Such 'impact' and 'success' agendas share a fundamental view of research and education as only worthwhile when measured in economic terms. There are differences, too. In the US, the funding for higher education is steadily and sharply declining without regard to measures, whereas in the UK, funding for higher education overall is somewhat more assured, although the distribution of it is tied to performance measures and increasing burden is placed on students to underwrite the costs.

In response to the increasing pressures of audit culture and the rising tide of metrics in academia in the UK, some researchers are pushing back (Wilsdon et al, 2015). In June 2014, two British professors of international politics, Meera Sabaratnam and Paul Kirby, wrote about why metrics are inappropriate for assessing research quality (Sabaratnam and Kirby, 2014). They argue that the metrics used in the REF, including Garfield's journal impact factor, are not accurately measuring research quality. They also point out that such a system 'systematically discriminate[s] against less established scholars', who are less likely to have high citation counts. Relying on citation indices, like the ones Garfield created, also disadvantages work by women and ethnic minorities, because their work is less likely to be cited (Sabaratnam and Kirby, 2014). They note that the putatively 'objective' measures like citation counts are 'highly vulnerable to gaming and manipulation' through practices like coercive citations (Sabaratnam and Kirby, 2014). The overall effects of using citations as a proxy for either 'impact' or 'quality' would be 'extremely deleterious to the standing and quality of UK academic research as a whole', they conclude. While Sabaratnam and Kirby report an overwhelmingly positive response to their activist blog post, there are other, more damaging unintended consequences from audit culture.

There is growing evidence that the emphasis on metrics is having a crushing effect on some academics. Scholars can feel an enormous individual pressure to produce publications and to win grants in order to satisfy the metrics of impact at their institution. In one tragic case, the emphasis on measuring scholarly impact cost the life of Stefan Grimm. A well-regarded and well-published scholar in toxicology at Imperial College London, Grimm committed suicide after being placed on 'performance review' following the news that his grant applications did not get funded (Parr, 2014). The reliance on a narrow range of metrics is prompting those scholars who want to have children to consider what this will mean for their research track records. In the context of an increasingly neoliberal university, where every activity is audited, some raise the provocative question: 'How many papers is a baby worth?' (Klocker and Drozdzewski, 2012). To be sure, these are symptoms of larger global processes of neoliberal economic and political policies and not merely the result of Garfield's citation analysis tools. But his tools have had some profound, if unintended, consequences for measuring scholarly impact in the academy.

For over three decades, ISI, under Garfield's leadership, produced and marketed a wide range of information management tools. In 1988, Garfield sold ISI to a mid-sized publishing company for a reported $24 million. Then, in 1992, ISI was sold again for $210 million to multi-billion-dollar media conglomerate Thomson Reuters (Lane, 1992). Since he developed them in the middle of the 20th century, Garfield's citation analysis tools, originally intended to spot scientific trends and map the flow of ideas, have become widely institutionalized to evaluate scholarly impact. These tools have then become privatized and monetized, most recently by Thomson Reuters. What this means is that now, in order to access these tools, academic libraries pay a hefty fee to Thomson Reuters for academic review committees to be able to use them.

The dominance of Garfield's tools in measuring scholarly impact disrupted a previous system of evaluation that relied solely on reputation and personal relationship. This resulted in institutions filled with 'administrators instead of world-class scientists', as Garfield explained (interview by Istvan Hargittai, October 1999). Yet, the system of citation analysis and indices that he developed is subject to manipulation through a variety of means, including coercive citation practices. When used on its own and not in combination with peer evaluation, citation analysis can reproduce existing hierarchies within academia by systematically disadvantaging everyone except white men from elite institutions, who are more likely to cite themselves and each other.

Garfield's tools are also effectively behind a paywall at Thomson Reuters; knowingly or not, academics 'pay' to use them as a benefit of their university library affiliations. Now, the dominant practices that have developed in tandem with Garfield's citation analysis tools that are being disrupted by digital media technologies.

As the application of Garfield's tools suggests, new technologies and open scholarship cannot disrupt traditional patterns of citation without a steady intention to shift the infrastructure of our scholarly systems. Veletsianos and Kimmons argue that 'merely developing digital literacies … does not mean that scholars will necessarily become efficient or equal participants in online spaces' (Veletsianos and Kimmons, 2012). We must apply open scholarship and digital practices to circulate ideas from the scholarly margins as well as those from the disciplinary mainstream. We must aim to create rich and varied open resources and practices to support intersectional scholarly work that unsettles methods and assumptions. We must conscientiously critique our scholarly tools and assessment patterns. Without new ways of assigning value to scholarship, we will perpetuate dominant systems of thought at the expense of innovation and creativity. The conditions that constrain attention to some ideas and support attention for others cannot be addressed with technology alone; they require social and political adjustments.

The flow of scholarly information is becoming more open. The fact that academic work, even that behind paywalls, is searchable by Google Scholar at relatively low cost is an important shift and one that promises to reconfigure evaluative practices in the academy (Lamont,

2012). We are just at the beginning of understanding how digital media technologies will transform the way we measure scholarly impact in the academy. When asked about how the Internet was changing scholarly impact, Garfield replied with another question of his own: 'The Internet is having an impact but how would you measure it?' (Hargittai, 1999, p. 26).

Digital media and the rise of altmetrics

Jason Priem and an international group of collaborators have some ideas about how to measure scholarly impact in the digital era. In 2010, Priem, along with Dario Taraborelli, Paul Groth, and Cameron Neylon, drafted a 'manifesto' calling for 'more tools and research based on altmetrics' (Priem et al, 2010). Altmetrics, as they explain, is an alternative form of metric – hence, 'altmetric' – that reflects the changing flows of scholarly information in the digital era better than Garfield's citation analysis. They explain the need for altmetrics this way:

> No one can read everything. We rely on filters to make sense of the scholarly literature, but the narrow, traditional filters are being swamped. However, the growth of new, online scholarly tools allows us to make new filters; these altmetrics reflect the broad, rapid impact of scholarship in this burgeoning ecosystem. We call for more tools and research based on altmetrics. (Priem et al, 2010)

Rather than the journal-based metric of Garfield's JIF, altmetrics enable article-level measurement, which better reflects the way scholars search and find information. Typically, we find, read, and use an article based on discovery through specific search terms, and altmetrics can reflect that. Unlike the citation metrics that Garfield developed, altmetrics will track the spread of ideas outside the academy, including circulation in sources that are not peer-reviewed. Priem and colleagues argue that altmetrics are less susceptible to manipulation than the JIF. In effect, they suggest using the statistical power of big data to algorithmically detect work that is being cited across a wide array of platforms, not only in academic journals. Some academics are excited about altmetrics, in the hope that this new set of metrics will provide an innovative way to measure scholarly impact (Matthews, 2015).

'If you want people to find and read your research, build up a digital presence in your discipline, and use it to promote your work when you have something interesting to share. It's pretty darn obvious, really', suggests Melissa Terras. Terras trained in art history, her research focuses on using computational techniques to enable research in the arts and humanities that would otherwise be impossible. She became curious about the way social media is affecting the dissemination of her work, and decided to conduct an experiment.

Terras had posted her papers in her institutional repository, but she could see that most had only one or two downloads. She decided to find out what would happen if she blogged and tweeted about them. Terras discovered that her scholarly papers that were mentioned on social media had at least more than 11 times the number of downloads than similar papers that were not. Upon blogging and tweeting, within 24 hours, there were, on average, 70 downloads. One paper of hers in particular was downloaded over a thousand times in the year following her social media experiment. Her paper became the sixteenth most downloaded paper in the entire institutional repository in the final quarter of 2011. This paper was also the most downloaded paper in 2011 in *LLC Journal*, where it was published, with 376 full-text downloads (Terras, 2012).

Terras' experiment, with her 376 full-text downloads, is an example of the different approach to measuring scholarly impact that is implicit in altmetrics. She demonstrated the power of social media to boost readership of her work and she has data to support this. Her experiment also highlights the article as the unit of analysis, typical of altmetrics, rather than the journal, as with the JIF. Terras' experiment was conducted in the spirit of Boyer's notion of the scholarship of engagement, and a clear example of the scholarship of sharing knowledge. She wanted people to find her work and read it – and they did. But what Terras' experiment and the rise of altmetrics do not yet do is to reach back into the academy.

At the time of writing, we do not know of any colleges or universities that officially use altmetrics in the tenure and promotion process. However, traditional journals incorporate evidence from altmetrics of wider readership into their journal's online interface. Grant funders are very interested in alternative measures of influence and reach that incorporate social media data.

In many ways, the rise of altmetrics speaks to the kind of change that Kathleen Fitzpatrick evokes concerning peer review in the digital era: that it is transforming from a process focused on gatekeeping to one concerned with filtering the wealth of scholarly material made available via the Internet (Fitzpatrick, 2010). In other words, instead of producing knowledge in a context in which knowledge is rare and hard to access, now scholars are creating knowledge in a context of abundance and information overload (Shenk, 1997; Stewart, 2015). Altmetrics is a way to measure impact that takes into account these new filtering systems, like search engines and article downloads. Whether or not altmetrics will truly disrupt Garfield's citation analysis tools remains to be seen, but Garfield's career is still relevant here.

The story of Eugene Garfield's unintended influence on how we measure scholarly impact may turn out to be something of a cautionary tale for the digital era and the rise of altmetrics. 'After five years, we still don't have much of an idea of what we're measuring', Juan Pablo Alperin told a room full of altmetrics enthusiasts at a conference in Amsterdam (Matthews, 2015). Alperin, a professor at Simon Fraser University in Canada, is an expert in online scholarly communications and how we measure it. Alperin voiced concerns that altmetrics might lead to the creation of a new, all-encompassing metric that merely replaced citation-based measurement. 'Aren't we going down the same route [with altmetrics]?', he asked (Matthews, 2015). If altmetrics becomes enclosed and monetized, then it will be going down the same route as Garfield's citation analysis tools. To escape from this same route, we have to rethink engagement.

From impact to engagement

Returning to Boyer's concept of scholarly engagement and Stewart's analysis of this for the digital era might suggest how we might think differently about scholarly impact. Stewart contends that digitally networked scholarship makes a difference in how scholarly communities, whether institutions or entire disciplines, understand and honor the values of scholarly inquiry that presume a context of scarcity of knowledge, when scholarship is now being done in a context of information abundance (Stewart, 2015). If abundance and openness are the context of contemporary scholarship, and Boyer's typology is the guiding principle for how we think about impact, then engagement might look very different.

Open syllabus metadata

The citation analysis tools SCI, SSCI and JIF only function within the universe of journal articles and cannot be used to measure the impact of books or other kinds of scholarly work. If one were to imagine a broader view of scholarly engagement that included books and found a way to measure how widely read (or at least assigned) they were across college campuses, then you might have something like the Open Syllabus Project.[3]

The Open Syllabus Project finds course syllabi available on the open web and looks for which books are being assigned in US college classes. To date, the project has collected over one million syllabi, and has extracted citations and other metadata from them. The Open Syllabus team collects metadata – there is no individual or personally identifying information in their database. It is open for everyone to explore. 'Such data has many uses. For academics, for example, it offers a window onto something they generally know very little about: how widely their work is read', says one of the developers behind the project (Karaganis and McClure, 2016).

The Open Syllabus Project allows for a new kind of publication metric based on the frequency with which books are taught, which the developers are calling a 'teaching score': 'The score is derived from the ranking order of the text, not the raw number of citations, such that a book or article that is used in four or five classes gets a score of one, while Plato's *The Republic*, which is assigned 3,500 times, gets a score of 100' (Karaganis and McClure, 2016). The results from their initial analysis are promising in terms of the wider range of voices represented in the classroom. In US courses covering fiction from the last 50 years, the most frequently taught book is Toni Morrison's *Beloved*, followed by William Gibson's *Neuromancer*, Art Spiegelman's *Maus*, Toni Morrison's *The bluest eye*, Sandra Cisneros' *The house on Mango Street*, Anne Moody's *Coming of age in Mississippi*, Leslie Marmon Silko's *Ceremony* and Alice Walker's *The color purple* (Karaganis and McClure, 2016).

The developers behind the Open Syllabus Project are clear in tying their project to the idea of scholarly engagement and a different way of measuring impact:

> If you like the idea of a more publicly engaged academy, you need to look elsewhere for incentives. That's where we think our 'teaching score' metric could be useful. Teaching captures a very different set of judgments about what is

important than publication does. In particular, it accords more value to qualities that are useful in the classroom, like accessibility and clarity. A widely taught but infrequently cited article is an important achievement, but an invisible one to current impact metrics. (Karaganis and McClure, 2016)

If having students in college classes engage with your work is one priority for rethinking scholarly engagement, so, too, is reconsidering the relationship between universities and the communities that surround and support them.

University–community engagement

Kristine Miller is interested in design and neighborhoods, but she found the usual approach lacking. 'A lot of times in design programs, people tend to improve places sort of expecting "new and better" people to move in, while our question was, how can our professions make neighborhoods better for the people who live there currently?' (Miller, quoted in Hinterberg, 2015).

Miller is a professor at the University of Minnesota, where she experiments with ways to open scholarly impact to other kinds of evaluation in line with Boyer's scholarship of engagement. The University of Minnesota is developing a set of Public Engagement Metrics for their faculty. These include measures such as: evidence of application of research findings by communities and evidence of the contribution of public engagement to student learning. As part of this initiative, the University of Minnesota gives awards to faculty who are doing exemplary work in community engagement, including Kristine Miller, who received an award in 2015.

In 2005, Miller began a collaboration with Juxtaposition Arts as part of a partnership called Remix, with the goal to make the design of cities more equitable for the people who live in them: 'I want all of my students to find that sweet spot between what they're really good at and the change that they want to see in the world. And I think that engaged scholarship is a really way good way of doing that' (Miller, quoted in Hinterberg, 2015). When reflecting on the success of the project, Miller talks about relationships:

> Our success can really be measured in the people who are coming out of our program and the relationships that we've

123

developed. It's exciting now, 10 years into it, to see the next generation, to see students who have come through our program taking on roles in the Twin Cities and elsewhere drawing attention to equity issues. (Hinterberg, 2015)

The kind of work Miller is doing is a collaborative project, one that involves a large number of people – both students and people in the community – over a long period of time. In traditional measures of scholarly impact, Miller's community engagement work would be discounted in favor of the number of citations she has and the impact factor of the journals in which she has published. Shifting to a paradigm of engagement, and finding ways to reward it, makes this important kind of work legible within the academy.

Transactional and transformational metrics

Transactional metrics include both traditional academic measures of impact (such as citations), and alternative measures (like altmetrics such as downloads or mentions on social media). Quantitative transactional measures of impact can also include lasting social change, such as changes to public policy. One of the useful aspects about this conceptualization is that it illustrates the incremental change that altmetrics represent. In other words, altmetrics are just another way of counting things – downloads and social media mentions, rather than citations – but it's still just counting things. Counting and quantification can tell us some things, but it doesn't provide a whole picture of scholarly engagement.

On the 'transformational' side are those things that it is difficult, perhaps even impossible, to measure, but that are so crucial to doing work that has a lasting impact. These include identifying allies, building relationships, establishing collaborations, and co-creating projects. Ultimately, transformational work is about changing lives, changing the broader cultural narrative, and changing society in ways that make it more just and democratic for all. These kinds of transformations demand a different kind of metric, one that relies primarily on storytelling. How might this work in academia? Well, to some extent, it already does.

To take the example of teaching, you may have got the advice 'save everything' for your tenure file. This advice often goes something like, 'every time a student sends you a thank you card, or writes you an email, or says, "this class made all the difference for me", save that for your tenure file'. That's part of how we 'finish the symphony', to borrow Doug Howard's metaphor; we get notes from students and we compile those into a narrative about our teaching (Howard, 2014). It's impartial, to be sure, but it's something. The comments that students add to teaching evaluations are another place where we see impact in narrative form,[4] although these are so skewed by the context of actually sitting in the class that it misses the longer-term impact of how that course may have changed someone.

For the diminishing few with tenure, those letters of recommendation we write in support of junior scholars are another example of the use of narrative in evaluation. Whether we are writing for someone to get hired, promoted, or granted tenure, what we are doing when we craft those letters is creating a narrative about the candidate's impact on their corner of the academic world so far. Of course, we augment that with quantitative data, 'this many articles over this span of time', and 'these numbers in teaching evaluations'. The fact is, we already combine transactional and transformational metrics in academia in the way that we do peer evaluations. What we need to consider in academia is expanding how we think about 'impact' and realize the way that we already use both quantitative and qualitative measures to evaluate and assess the impact of our work.

Our (mostly failed) experiment with metrics

Given the context of the neoliberal university, raising the subject of metrics can set off alarm bells for faculty, who are right to be concerned about measures of output being used to demolish scholarship and subvert tenure (Holmwood, 2011, 2014). We ran into some of this resistance when we tried to incorporate a survey about metrics with our project.

Our idea was to do a simple pre- and post-test assessment of the increase (we hoped) in social media use and mainstream media mentions of faculty research. We would do this by sending a brief survey to the faculty, ask about their engagement with social media, and then track both social media use and mainstream media mentions. As an academic institution, ours is quite unique in structure. There is a small cohort of faculty (around 150) appointed exclusively at the Graduate Center, which is the PhD-granting arm of CUNY, and nearly all the faculty in the disciplines have tenure. Many are 'distinguished' faculty (the rank above full professor), and most are very prominent scholars in senior stages of their careers. There is a much larger group of doctoral faculty (around 1,800), who have a primary appointment at one of the 24 campuses of CUNY and also have joint appointments at the Graduate Center. This consortial model of a university means many things, but one artifact of our organizational structure is that there is no way to send an all-faculty email across the consortium.

Our plan was to begin by surveying just the smaller group of central faculty, then extend the survey to the affiliated doctoral faculty. Informal discussions with faculty about the idea of the survey raised concerns because our project had the support of the Provost's office. A number of faculty members balked at the mere suggestion of completing such a survey; another faculty member suggested that this was an indication of a larger trend of 'metrification' in higher education and wanted nothing to do with it. Still another faculty member predicted a low response rate on anything coming from the Provost's office. Internally, a debate ensued about who might send out the survey to minimize the fact that it did have the endorsement of the Provost. Eventually, we abandoned the idea altogether and chalked it up to one of the many lessons learned about the limits of top-down change in an institution with an empowered faculty.

At the same time we met with this resistance, we were busy training scholars in the MediaCamp workshops in a variety of hybrid, digital skills (see Chapter Five). The people who came to our workshops evidenced a larger trend within academia. Increasingly, scholars are using digital media technologies to do their work, collaborate and find others who share their research interests (Lupton, 2014; Carrigan, 2016a). Scholars who are immersed in digital media technologies expect this work to count when it comes to decisions about hiring and tenure (Starkman, 2013; Matthew, 2016). The reality that digitally fluent scholars confront in most institutions is one in which legacy measures of scholarly impact are deeply entrenched. At this time, there are no good ways to measure scholarly engagement in ways that are equitable across disciplines and legible across all institutions of higher education.

Forward thinking: the humane ends of scholarship

We began this chapter with a discussion of Boyer's scholarship of engagement. For Boyer, universities and colleges were among 'the greatest sources of hope for intellectual and civic progress' (Boyer, 1996). We tend to agree. There is so much possibility in the work of scholars to address social inequality in all its dimensions. In discussing the scholarship of engagement, Boyer said: 'The issue, then, ... is not whether scholarship will be applied but whether the work of scholars will be directed toward humane ends' (Boyer, 1996). In our view, it is this idea of the 'humane ends' of scholarship that may provide a way forward in thinking about how to measure scholarly impact through a metric not based on citation analysis but on social justice.

'In the century ahead, higher education in this country has an urgent obligation to become more vigorously engaged in the issues of our day' (Boyer, 1996, p. 28). On campuses like the University of Missouri this past year, the 'most pressing issues of the day' has been #BlackLivesMatter. The movement began as a hashtag to raise awareness about the death of Trayvon Martin and the extrajudicial killing of black people across the US. When a recent high school graduate, Michael Brown, was shot and killed by a white police officer in Ferguson, Missouri, and his body left on a hot, August pavement for hours, protestors took to the streets and mobilized online using a variety of hashtags including #BlackLivesMatter, #Ferguson and #MikeBrown. At the nearby University of Missouri, just an hour-and-a-half away by car from Ferguson, students began 'MU for Mike Brown', a Black Lives Matter-affiliated group formed in solidarity with the uprisings over the shooting to death of an unarmed teenager.

Solidarity with the #BlackLivesMatter protest group gave rise to a second group, Concerned Student 1-9-5-0, a reference to the year 1950, when black students were first admitted to the University of Missouri (Izadi, 2015). These students were spurred to action by a pattern of racial harassment they experienced on their campus, such as a swastika drawn in excrement on a campus building, shouts of the 'n-word' yelled from passing cars at African American students, and a Legion of Black Collegians theater rehearsal disrupted by more racial slurs being yelled, along with a constant drumbeat of other incidents. In October, during a homecoming parade, students blocked University President Tim Wolfe's car, insisting that he respond to the series of racist incidents on campus. Wolfe expressed concern, but did not leave his car. A graduate student, Jonathan Butler, released a list of demands and began a hunger strike. At the top of the list of demands was that Wolfe resign, and that any replacement be chosen through a collaborative process. Also among the demands were: 'We demand that by the academic year 2017-2018, the University of Missouri increases the percentage of black faculty and staff campus-wide to 10%' and develop a strategic plan to 'improve retention rates' among marginalized students by changing the campus environment (Concerned Student 1-9-5-0, 2015). The predominantly African American football team, along with white teammates and coach, also joined the calls for the president to resign and threatened not to play until he did so (Green, 2015). If the football players went on strike, the University of Missouri would stand to lose millions in football-generated revenue. On November 9, Tim Wolfe resigned (Eligon and Pérez-Peña, 2015).

Part of what the students at the University of Missouri did was to change the conversation about metrics to ones that mattered to them. Instead of the metrics about productivity or student success, they started a different conversation about social justice metrics. The relevant metrics had to do with the white dominance of higher education, and their experience of campus life in particular, such as the number of times they got harassed on campus based on race or ethnicity (frequently), and the number of faculty who are people of color (fewer than 10%). Within academia, the issue of the white dominance of higher education most frequently gets expressed as a 'lack of racial diversity among faculty', but this does not go nearly far enough to describe the current situation. Colleges and universities who want to fulfill Boyer's vision and be engaged in the 'most pressing issues of the day' are going to face an uphill struggle, given the pattern of systemic racism in US higher education.

Boyer's vision of colleges and universities as 'the most promising institutions for progress' is one that was premised on his narrative about land grants (issued by President Lincoln 'during the dark days of the Civil War' to help 'workers and farmers') and the GI Bill ('a wonderful experiment' of 'rising expectations' (Boyer, 1990). In fact, higher education in the US has never been a level playing field (Herbold, 1994). Although some 8 million veterans were able to take advantage of the GI Bill to access a college education, most African American veterans were not able to take advantage of this federal program to which they were fully entitled due to rampant discrimination on college and university campuses (Herbold, 1994). This was not a new development in the post-World War II era. As historian Craig Wilder chronicles in his book, *Ebony and Ivy* (2013), the leading universities in the US were built using the labor of enslaved people and were dependent on human bondage for their operation through the first half of the 19th century (Wilder, 2013). Understandably, this affected the production of knowledge at these same institutions as they became the sites for the development and sustenance of racist ideologies. The question before us is whether or not the university can become a place 'vigorously engaged in the issues of the day' when those issues are at the very heart of the inequality within the university itself.

Empowered, digitally networked faculty and students pose a serious challenge to the smooth management of the neoliberal university. Tim

Wolfe, in some ways, typifies the new management of the neoliberal university. He came to the University of Missouri from private industry, starting his career at IBM and eventually becoming president of Novell, a software company (Wilson, 2015). Part of what students (and some faculty) did at the University of Missouri was to use digital media technology to disrupt the business-as-usual operation of the university, much like ACT UP protestors did in the 1980s (see Chapter Four). They used the 'internet empires' that DeMillo warned make it difficult to govern a university, and in this, he is correct. Another component to their challenge to the neoliberal university was to effectively change the most relevant metrics at hand. This is part of what the students at the University of Missouri and other campuses did in the fall of 2015 – they changed the metrics being discussed. If we reimagine a world in which higher education is engaged in trying to end inequality rather than continuing as an engine of it, then we might imagine different kinds of metrics, ones that assess how a particular institution is addressing the social inequality around it.

We return to where we began this chapter, with Boyer's call to a scholarship of engagement. For Boyer, the call to be engaged scholars is not an end in itself, but one that propels us toward the 'humane ends of scholarship' (Boyer, 1996). It is this idea that may provide a way forward in thinking about how to measure scholarly impact through a metric not based on citation analysis but on social justice. However, we recognize that such a reconceptualization of metrics is wholly at odds with the logics of the neoliberal university and the politics of austerity. But it is possible to confront these, as the students at the University of Missouri have taught us. We would argue that it is imperative that we follow their lead for the sake of higher education.

In many ways, the student protestors and their list of metric-embedded demands are making colleges and universities more 'vigorously engaged in the issues of our day' – to use Boyer's phrase – and more politically relevant than they have been since the 1960s. Jennifer Wilson, a postdoctoral fellow at the University of Pennsylvania, put it this way: 'At a time when the value of a college education, particularly a humanities education, is under attack, the Black Lives Matter campus protesters of 2015 have shown, through their own display of historically informed and intersectional politics, that universities matter' (Wilson, 2015). To move toward the humane ends of scholarship and be vigorously engaged in the issues of the day, we urgently need to change the conversation about metrics to one that enables us to think about the university in relation to social inequality.

Notes

1   See www.ascb.org/dora
2   See www.ref.ac.uk
3   See http://opensyllabusproject.org/
4   Of course, the use of student evaluations as reliable metrics is contentious. The comments from disgruntled students can have a negative impact on faculty careers. Research has consistently shown that the race and gender of the professor have a significant impact on students' assessment of faculty. See, for example, Anderson and Smith (2005).

SEVEN

The future of being
a scholar

The renowned science fiction author Octavia Butler, after writing 11 novels about the future, concluded that predicting the future is difficult:

> Some of the most mistaken predictions I've seen are simply, 'In the future, we will have more and more of whatever's holding our attention right now.' If we're in a period of prosperity, then in the future, prosperity it will be. If we're in a period of recession, we're doomed to even greater distress. (Butler, 2000)

We are mindful of Butler's observation as we consider the future of being a scholar.

Imagining a future in which there is a turnover all at once from legacy to digital models of scholarship is unhelpful in thinking about the changes afoot. Indeed, thinking of legacy and digital scholarship as binary risks committing a type of 'digital dualism' (Jurgenson, 2012). Digital dualism is a habit of thinking that conceives the online and offline to be largely distinct and separate. This way of thinking perpetuates a myth of cyberspace as someplace out there, away from real life (Rey, 2012).

A common (mis)understanding created by this way of thinking is that lived experience is zero-sum: that time spent online means less spent offline (Jurgenson, 2012). Embracing this kind of dualism is to overlook the ways that the digital and the material are imbricated, the way they overlap in everyday life (Sassen, 2002; Wajcman, 2002). In the digital era, we are no longer merely consumers of media nor only producers; we have become *prosumers* – both producers and consumers at the same time (Ritzer and Jurgenson, 2010). So it is with scholarship.

The future of being a scholar will include using a *bricolage* of digital practices, which will continue to change. As just one example, take the way in which reading is changing. If a scholar reads a printed book to understand the argument and then goes online to search that same book for keywords, authors cited, and page numbers of a particular passage, that scholar is engaging in both legacy and digital scholarly practices. University presses and other book publishers may catch up to this scholarly hybrid use of text by offering different versions of a volume for a lower price, but that day is not yet here. It may very well be the case that once publishers catch up to this practice, scholars and readers of all kinds will have moved on to different technologies that suit their needs more fully. As another example, perhaps more commonplace, consider the card catalogs that have now been almost entirely replaced (in North American and European academic libraries, at least) by databases and search engines, shifting researchers from analog to digital practice. Today, being a scholar means having to navigate through overlapping legacy and digital models of scholarship that can seem like two different worlds. In the not-too-distant future, we will not find the digital worth remarking on, because it will be so ordinary. Such predictions have affective repercussions.

'Superstition, depression and fear play major roles in our efforts at prediction', suggests Octavia Butler about the way emotions influence our ability to imagine the future (Butler, 2000). While the Internet may trigger excited, happy feelings about the possibility of exploring new realms for some, for others, the rise of digital media technologies can signal loss, longing and affection for another time.

This confluence of emotional reactions is similar to those evoked by artist Ann Hamilton's public artwork for the San Francisco Public Library (Hamilton, 2015). When the new library opened in 1996, keyboards and computer terminals supplanted the card catalog, and Hamilton's spectacular installation uses the artifacts of the displaced system to make art. She took 50,000 individual paper cards from the catalog and, working with 200 artist collaborators, annotated each one with a quote from the book referenced on the card. Taken together, the cards make up a dramatic display at the entrance to the library that suggests 'the reverie of reading and researching'. When a friend and academic colleague of ours first encountered Hamilton's public art project, "I just wept," she says. For her, the demise of the card catalog brought a great sadness. The keyboards and screens seemed like a cold replacement for the warmth and tactile pleasure of wooden drawers and paper cards. For scholars who came of age before the Internet, like our friend, the transformation from legacy to digital practices can feel like a loss. Yet, for the generation of scholars that come after us, wooden drawers full of paper cards don't carry this emotional valance. Instead, drawers full of cards simply seem like a terribly inefficient way to search for information. While the memories of browsing a library with wooden cases of paper cards may fill some of us with nostalgia for our own emergence as scholars, we can't let this obscure our clear vision of the changes happening to knowledge production and what this means for the future of being a scholar.

Digital media technologies make it easier to create hybrid projects across fields that are typically separate. The future of being a scholar will include more blending of academia, journalism, and documentary filmmaking, particularly around activism. Our particular experiment was to bring together scholars, activists, journalists, and documentary filmmakers around specific topics in order to focus public attention on these issues, forge new partnerships, and create new knowledge through a series of summits, podcasts, and allied open access eBooks. Digital media technologies make possible new kinds of collaborations, and the future of being a scholar will be more collaborative. It will include more collaborations between journalists and academics, such as the one that Louis Paul of *The Guardian* and Tim Newburn of the London School of Economics created with their project *Reading the Riots* (see Chapter Two). As Newburn remarked about academics, 'we have a lot to learn from journalism' (Devine et al, 2013). Yet, for scholars who want to learn the skills of contemporary journalism or documentary filmmaking, at the present time there are scant opportunities to do so.

Digital media training for academics is still missing at most institutions, and those who want to learn are mostly left on their own to become autodidacts. Our experiment was an intra-institutional partnership to offer free, open classes in digital media technologies to academics and activists. The CUNY Graduate School of Journalism had an existing set of courses designed for journalists making transition from legacy to digital, and we took those same workshops and modified them slightly to make them more relevant for the rest of academia. These proved popular with faculty and graduate students, activists, and those working in non-governmental organizations, as well as with administrative staff at the university. Academic institutions benefit from the use of digital media by faculty, graduate students, and staff. Administrative staff use digital media technologies to promote degrees, departments, and programs, and to recruit and retain students. When faculty and graduate students share their research on social media alongside their institutional affiliation, they boost the profile and reputation of the university. Forward-thinking academic institutions of the future will find ways to offer such training for scholars, particularly if they want scholars engaged in the public sphere.

For scholars who want to have an impact beyond the academy, the scholarship of engagement is possible in new ways through digital media technologies (Boyer, 1996; Stewart, 2015a, 2015b). At the same time, the Internet makes it easier to reach wider publics, and it also makes it easier to measure reach in downloads, hits, views, and re-posts. These altmetrics influence conventional metrics of citations in peer-reviewed literature (Eysenbach, 2011; Priem et al, 2012).

The unintended consequence of Eugene Garfield's influence on the current use of flawed and controversial metrics may serve as a cautionary tale for those who are enthusiastic about the promise of metrics based on digital media to be truly alternative in any meaningful way. Our own experiment here with metrics failed, as we met with obstacles to even surveying faculty, who suspect that such measures can be used for punitive, neoliberal regimes such as the Research Excellence Framework (REF) in the UK. If the discussion of measuring scholarly impact remains within a framework of managerialism to ensure the smooth operation of the neoliberal university, then the future of being a scholar is grim indeed.

There are other ways of conceptualizing scholarly impact. A different approach to measuring scholarly impact is to focus on social justice metrics. If scholars in the future are to take seriously Boyer's call to 'vigorously engage in the issues of the day', then we will need to change the discussion about metrics to one that focuses on inequality (Boyer, 1996). Jonathan Butler and other students at the University of Missouri issued a list of demands that included social justice metrics. These social justice metrics were things like the demand that 10% of all faculty be people of color, and that there be a 10-year plan for retaining students of color. These social justice metrics, in combination with other protest strategies, were a way for Butler and other students to hold the administration at the University of Missouri accountable for the inequality within the institution.

Using metrics to highlight injustice and hold the powerful accountable is part of a longer tradition of social justice metrics that could be traced back to Ida B. Wells-Barnett, a journalist, scholar, and activist, who was the first to compile statistics about lynching when the US government was uninterested in such data collection (Giddings, 2008). Today, Samuel Sinyangwe is leading a team of data scientists, activists, and journalists, who are using digital media technologies to map police violence at a time when the US government is not collecting these data.[1] In the future, the discussion of scholarly impact will have to shift to social justice metrics, if we are to transform the neoliberal university.

These digital practices have a material, embodied basis as well as a political context, and these will shape the future. Being a scholar will mean confronting the inequality within higher education itself. This will depend a great deal on what the investment in faculty hiring will be and who will be included in those hires. Several things are true about the academy now: it is a white-dominated system in every sector (Supiano, 2015), there is less willingness to support higher education as a public good (Holmwood, 2011), and there are a declining number of full-time, tenure-track positions available to those with PhDs (Kendzior, 2014). This means that issues raised by the students at the University of Missouri and other campuses across the US in the fall of 2015 were not an aberration, but a harbinger of things to come. The inequality within the academy, and how this reflects the broader patterns of social inequality, will continue to be a feature of being a scholar. The future of being a scholar will, of necessity, have to encounter some constellation of these social facts. Of course, how you see that future depends entirely on where you are standing.

Where are you standing?

'It's also true that where we stand determines what we're able to see', writes Octavia Butler about predicting the future (Butler, 2000). Where we stand affects what we see when we consider the future of scholarly practice.

For those who stand in a place from which they want to remake universities and colleges into blueberry farms or widget factories, the rise of digital technologies seems to hold the promise of remedying the 'cost disease' of the labor-intensive project of higher education. From the standpoint of administrators who want to increase 'productivity' – by which they mean increasing the number of credentialed students in the shortest possible time to degree with the fewest number of faculty – the fantasy of MOOCs as a technological solution to the crisis of underfunding in higher education is appealing.

For faculty who often stand in classrooms and who appreciate participatory pedagogy, the digital turn means a future in which opening education is possible in new ways. For students who stand at the entrance to college, they will expect to encounter digital technologies in the classroom. They will enter college already immersed in a near ubiquitous digital media environment. Being a scholar in the classroom will mean guiding students to make critical sense of the digitally mediated environment in which we all find ourselves. From the standpoint of lifelong learners, there will be even more opportunities now to learn online. One ripple effect of the 'Year of the MOOC' is that it has renewed a wider interest in, and experimentation with, teaching in digitally networked environments. The MOOCs started by Siemens and Cormier have spawned dozens of non-corporate, faculty-driven experiments in different ways of teaching. From SMOCs to SPOCs to DOCCs to our own POOC (see Chapter Three), these scholar-designed learning environments have expanded the conversation about what it means to be a scholar in the digital era. Whether administrators, faculty, students or lifelong learners, where we stand affects what we see when we look to the future of scholarly practice.

For those who stand outside the academy, without official university affiliations, it may not seem as if there has been, or will be, much change in scholarly practice. Over the length of this project, we saw at first hand Robert Darnton's point about the iron gates with spikes protecting the university as a metaphor for the way scholarly publications are sealed behind paywalls (Darnton, 2012). This system keeps out a whole range of people who want to read academic work, from scholars in other hemispheres to students who have already graduated to the university's neighbors. Walling off knowledge like this even keeps out academic authors who have contributed their own words to those restricted journals (Tadween Editors, 2013).

Now, chrome turnstiles that require university IDs with electromagnetic strips to pass through them have replaced the iron spikes, but they are just as effective at barring outsiders from entering the academy. When we located our course in a specific neighborhood, our goal was to make a difference on our own campus, in the neighborhood and around the world – and in many ways we did that. Thousands of people from around the world participated in the course, and more importantly, people from the neighborhood connected with others in the course. The model of open access we forged with that course has become a standard against which others can measure their own degree of openness. With additional funding and an institutional commitment to continue, that neighborhood-focused course could be a permanent feature opening the university to the community. This sort of ongoing investment in the community and this endeavor would have gone a long way to address at least part of the well-deserved criticisms we heard from some in the community. However, even with a greater investment, we would still have to find a way to address the inequality of resources between the university and the neighborhood, and the very real ways in which the university is an enclosed space. Such a project will always have to confront the politics of land use, real estate, and the physical space of the campus building at a time when elected officials, campus administrators, and campus security are at odds with neighborhood residents. Where one stands matters in how one views the enclosure of the university.

Currently, the big five commercial publishers have a cartel-like grip on the ecosystem of scholarly publishing, charging exorbitant fees that are choking library budgets and creating a serials crisis, while holding scholarly societies and associations in their grip through profit-sharing deals. Resistance to this legacy model of publishing is building. From 'declarations of independence' when entire editorial boards resign, such as those at *Lingua* did, to the formation of online and open journals such as *Cultural Anthropology*, there is a growing move toward throwing off the big five publishers and charting new paths toward open access. Where you stand in relation to the means of production of knowledge will change how you see the future of publishing.

People have always resisted this enclosure of the university and of knowledge. For one of us, the act of smuggling people into libraries was part of a commitment to the idea that access to information is a basic human right; for the other, someone asking, 'Why are you doing this work?' became a catalyst for rethinking the legacy model of scholarly publishing.

Forward thinking: investment, engagement, and a vibrant public sphere

The future of being a scholar relies in equal measure on the changes being wrought by the forces of commercialization and the shift toward digital models of scholarship. It is a common mistake to conflate the struggle between commercialization and democratization with the transformation from legacy to digital forms of scholarly practice. Too often academics want to resist commercialization by refusing the digital. In our view, this is a misplaced refusal that reflects a misunderstanding of the forces at play. If we take at face value that the goal of colleges and universities is to promote an enlightened citizenry, then what must lie ahead must be to challenge the status quo and transform being a scholar in ways that align with the pressing needs of a democratic society (Saltmarsh and Hartley, 2011).

From where we stand, the future of being a scholar will increasingly include various forms of digitally engaged resistance to the neoliberal war on higher education. At the same time that there are powerful forces aligned against the academy, scholars have amazing new opportunities to do their work in ways that matter to wider publics. A decisive step for scholars who want to become more engaged with digital media is to own the content of their own professional identity online. For many scholars, their only digital presence is a page on a departmental website that they have no control over and could not change or update even if they wanted to do so. A 'domain of one's own' that you can manage independently of any institution is crucial (Udell, 2012). From there, other possibilities emerge.

Scholars are beginning to demand that they own their work, whether books, journal articles, or the journals themselves. Groups like the Authors Alliance[2] offer scholarly authors guidance on how to get the rights to their work back from publishers. Opening access to academic work in turn makes with collaborators across sectors, between and among scholars, activists, journalists, documentary filmmakers, and other artists. Such collaborations will play an important role in the future of being a scholar. Owning one's own work also means that it can be shared with students in the classroom.

Being a scholar in the digitally networked classroom means guiding students to new knowledge and helping them become lifelong learners. Digital technologies make opening up the process of learning easier, and it can enlist students in the creation of knowledge and in their own learning. As scholars align with students through participatory pedagogy, the shared position of faculty and students within the machinery of the academy is an inevitable topic of concern. As student debt climbs to historic levels and faculty positions are increasingly precarious, these interests find a natural alliance against the corporatization of the university, and of course, digital media technologies can amplify and grow such an alliance.

We foresee a future in which digitally networked activism about academia – both within our institutions, pushing back on efforts that expand commercialization, and outside those institutions – plays an ever-increasing role. Scholars and students will become energized to demand that elected officials fully fund this public good or risk the disappearance of scholarly life altogether.

Our experiment was possible because of the investment of a philanthropic foundation, and it offered a clear vision of what might be if there were a broader commitment to substantial investing in the public good by municipal, state, and federal governments and by foundations. These kinds of institutions responsive to metrics, and what we can imagine is a future in which social justice metrics – like the ones the students at the University of Missouri used – will be applied to foundation boards, to college and university administrators, as well as to elected officials, to hold them accountable for persistent social inequality.

When Octavia Butler was asked to write a memorandum outlining her vision of the future, she chose to write about the importance of education in her life. 'I was poor, Black, the daughter of a shoeshine man and a maid', Butler explains. About her ambition, and society's reaction to it, she says: 'At best I was treated with gentle condescension when I said I wanted to be a writer'. She grew up to be an acclaimed author of science fiction novels and a MacArthur 'Genius Grant' award winner. She was certain about what made her achievement possible: 'Without the excellent, free public education that I was able to take advantage of, I might have found other things to do with my deferred dreams and stunted ambitions' (Butler, 2000).

The future of being a scholar will have to find a way to encourage the next Octavia Butlers, the next geniuses who will help us to imagine new worlds. Otherwise, why are we doing this work?

Notes

[1]   See http://mappingpoliceviolence.org/
[2]   See www.authorsalliance.org

References

AAUP (American Association of University Professors) Research Office (2013) *Trends in faculty employment status, 1975-2011.* Washington, DC (www.aaup.org/sites/default/files/Faculty_Trends_0.pdf).

Abel, R., Newlin, L. W., Strauch, K. P. and Strauch, B. (2002) *Scholarly publishing: Books, journals, publishers, and libraries in the twentieth century.* New York: Wiley.

Accardi, M. T., Drabinski, E. and Kumbier, A. (eds) (2010) *Critical library instruction: Theories and methods.* Duluth, MN: Library Juice Press.

Anderson, C. W. (2013) *Rebuilding the news: Metropolitan journalism in the digital age.* Philadelphia, PA: Temple University Press.

Anderson, K. J. and Smith, G. (2005) 'Students' preconceptions of professors: Benefits and barriers according to ethnicity and gender', *Hispanic Journal of Behavioral Sciences*, 27(2), pp. 184–201.

Anderson, T. (2013) 'Open access scholarly publications as OER', *The International Review of Research in Open and Distributed Learning*, 14(2), pp. 81–95.

Andrist, L., Chepp, V., Dean, P. and Miller, M. V. (2014) 'Toward a video pedagogy: A teaching typology with learning goals', *Teaching Sociology*, 42(3), pp. 196–206.

Anselmo, K. (2015) 'With academia moving in a digital direction, sustained investment in media training would benefit all', *LSE The Impact Blog*, October 22 (http://blogs.lse.ac.uk/impactofsocialsciences/2015/01/28/digital-academia-sustained-investment-media-training/).

Armstrong, T. (2006) 'Digital is forever', *Info/Law*, October 17(https://blogs.harvard.edu/infolaw/2006/10/17/digital-is-forever/).

Bauder, D. (2007) 'Private pain fuels HBO addiction docs', *Boston Globe*, March 13(www.boston.com/ae/tv/articles/2007/03/13/private_pain_fuels_hbo_addiction_docs/).

Beetham, H. and Sharpe, R. (2013) *Rethinking pedagogy for a digital age: Designing for 21st century learning.* New York: Routledge.

Bensman, S. J. (2013) 'Eugene Garfield, Francis Narin, and PageRank: The theoretical bases of the Google search engine', *arXiv:1312.3872 [cs.IR]* (http://arxiv.org/abs/1312.3872).

Bergstrom, T. C., Courant, P. N., McAfee, R. P. and Williams, M. A. (2014) 'Evaluating big deal journal bundles', *Proceedings of the National Academy of Sciences*, 111(26), pp. 9425–30.

Bernard, R. M., Abrami, P. C., Lou, Y., Borokhovski, E., Wade, A., Wozney, L., Wallet, P. A. et al (2004) 'How does distance education compare with classroom instruction? A meta-analysis of the empirical literature', *Review of Educational Research*, 74(3), pp. 379–439.

Best, J. (2015) 'Following the money across the landscape of sociology journals', *The American Sociologist*, pp. 1–16.

Blattman, C. (2015) *Ezra Klein: How researchers are terrible communicators, and how they can do better* (http://chrisblattman.com/2015/11/05/ezra-klein-how-researchers-are-terrible-communicators-and-how-they-can-do-better/).

Borgman, C. (2007) *Scholarship in the digital age: Information, infrastructure, and the Internet*. Cambridge, MA: The MIT Press.

Bosch, S. and Henderson, K. (2015) 'Whole lotta shakin' goin' on: Periodicals price survey 2015', *Library Journal*, April 23 (http://lj.libraryjournal.com/2015/04/publishing/whole-lotta-shakin-goin-on-periodicals-price-survey-2015/).

Bowen, W. G. (2015) *Higher education in the digital age*. Princeton, NJ: Princeton University Press.

Bowen, W. G. and Rudenstine, N. L. (1992) *In pursuit of the PhD*. Princeton, NJ: Princeton University Press.

boyd, d. (2014a) *It's complicated: The social lives of networked teens*. New Haven, CT: Yale.

boyd, d. (2014b) 'What's behind the free pdf of "It's complicated" (no, no, not malware...)', *apophenia*, March 3 (www.zephoria.org/thoughts/archives/2014/03/03/its-complicated-open-access.html).

Boyer, E. L. (1990) *Scholarship reconsidered: Priorities of the professoriate*. Princeton, NJ: Carnegie Foundation for the Advancement of Teaching.

Boyer, E. L. (1996) 'The scholarship of engagement', *Bulletin of the American Academy of Arts and Sciences*, 49(7), pp. 18–33.

Brembs, B., Button, K. and Munafò, M. (2013) 'Deep impact: Unintended consequences of journal rank', *Frontiers in Human Neuroscience*, 7, p. 291.

Brescia, W. and Miller, M. T. (2007) 'Technology in higher education graduate programs', in Wright, D. and Miller, M. T. (eds) *Training higher education policy makers and leaders: A graduate program perspective.* Charlotte, NC: IAP, pp. 177–86.

Brienza, C. (2015) 'Publishing between profit and public value: Academic books and open access policies in the United Kingdom', *Northern Lights: Film & Media Studies Yearbook*, 13(1), pp. 65–81.

Brown, W. (2015) *Undoing the demos: Neoliberalism's stealth revolution.* Cambridge, MA: The MIT Press.

Butler, O. (1993) *Parable of the sower.* New York: Four Walls Eight Windows.

Butler, O. (2000) 'Brave new worlds: A few rules for predicting the future', *Essence*, 31(1), pp. 164-6.

Campbell, L., Newman, A. and Safransky, S. (2013) 'Uniting Detroiters: Coming together from the ground up', *AntipodeFoundation.org* (http://antipodefoundation.org/scholar-activist-project-awards/201213-recipients/sapa-1213-safransky/).

Carrigan, M. (2012) 'The workflow for continuous publishing and how it compares to "traditional" publishing', *Mark Carrigan's Blog*, March 3 (http://markcarrigan.net/2012/03/03/the-workflow-for-continuous-publishing-and-how-it-compares-to-traditional-publishing/).

Carrigan, M. (2015) 'Life in the accelerated academy: Anxiety thrives, demands intensify and metrics hold the tangled web together', *Impact of Social Sciences*, April 7 (http://blogs.lse.ac.uk/impactofsocialsciences/2015/04/07/life-in-the-accelerated-academy-carrigan/).

Carrigan, M. (2016a) *Social media for academics.* Thousand Oaks, CA: Sage Publications.

Carrigan, M. (2016b) 'Social media presence'. Email correspondence with J. Daniels.

Case, M. M. (1999) 'Community responds to proposals regarding the journals crisis', *ARL: A bimonthly report*, (204), pp. 7–10.

Chafkin, M. (2013) 'Udacity's Sebastian Thrun, godfather of free online education, changes course', *Fast Company*, November 14 (www.fastcompany.com/3021473/udacity-sebastian-thrun-uphill-climb).

Chenoweth, E. (2014) 'A note on academic (ir)relevance', *Political Violence @ a Glance*, February 17 (http://politicalviolenceataglance.org/2014/02/17/a-note-on-academic-irrelevance/).

Christensen, G., Steinmetz, A., Alcorn, B., Bennett, A., Woods, D. and Emanuel, E. J. (2013) *The MOOC phenomenon: Who takes massive open online courses and why?* Rochester, NY: Social Science Research Network (http://papers.ssrn.com/abstract=2350964).

Cirasella, J. and Thistlethwaite, P. (2016) 'Open Access and the Graduate Author: A Dissertation Anxiety Manual', in K. Smith (ed) *Open access and the future of academic libraries*. New York: Rowman & Littlefield.

Clark, D. (2012) 'Startup Udacity builds bankroll for online learning', *WSJ Blogs: Digits*, October 25 (http://blogs.wsj.com/digits/2012/10/25/startup-udacity-builds-bankroll-for-online-learning/).

Coates, T. (2014) 'The smartest nerd in the room', *The Atlantic*, January 6 (www.theatlantic.com/politics/archive/2014/01/the-smartest-nerd-in-the-room/282836/).

Coates, T. (2015) *Between the world and me*. New York: Random House Publishing Group.

College Board (2016) *Average estimated undergraduate budgets, 2015-16*. New York: College Board (http://trends.collegeboard.org/college-pricing/figures-tables/average-estimated-undergraduate-budgets-2015-16).

Concerned Student 1-9-5-0 (2015) *List of demands from Concerned Student 1950 group*, *Columbia Daily Tribune* (www.columbiatribune.com/list-of-demands-from-concerned-student-group/pdf_345ad844-9f05-5479-9b64-e4b362b4e155.html).

Cormier, D. and Siemens, G. (2010) 'The open course: Through the open door – open courses as research, learning, and engagement', *EDUCAUSE Review*, 45(4), p. 30.

Cottom, T. M. (2013) 'Talking MOOCs and 4profits at UC Irvine', *tressiemc*, May 15 (http://tressiemc.com/2013/05/15/talking-moocs-4profits-at-uc-irvine/).

Cottom, T. M. (2015) '"Who do you think you are?" When marginality meets academic microcelebrity', *Ada: A Journal of Gender, New Media, and Technology*, (7) (http://adanewmedia.org/2015/04/issue7-mcmillancottom/).

Courtney, K. K. (2013) 'The MOOC syllabus blues: Strategies for MOOCs and syllabus materials', *College & Research Libraries News*, 74(10), pp. 514–17.

CUNY Newswire (2011) 'When tuition at CUNY was free, sort of', October 12 (www1.cuny.edu/mu/forum/2011/10/12/when-tuition-at-cuny-was-free-sort-of/).

Daniels, J. (2009) *Cyber racism: White supremacy online and the new attack on civil rights*. Lanham, MD: Rowman & Littlefield.

Daniels, J. (2012) 'Digital video: Engaging students in critical media literacy and community activism', *Explorations in Media Ecology*, 10(1-2), pp. 137–47.

Daniels, J. (2013) 'From tweet to blog post to peer-reviewed article: How to be a scholar now', LSE Impact blog, September 25 (http://blogs.lse.ac.uk/impactofsocialsciences/2013/09/25/how-to-be-a-scholar-daniels/).

Daniels, J. (2014) 'Roundup of responses to Kristof's call for professors in the public sphere', *Just Publics @ 365*, February 19 (http://justpublics365.commons.gc.cuny.edu/02/2014/roundup-kristof-professors-public-sphere/).

Daniels, J. and Feagin, J. R. (2011) 'The (coming) social media revolution in the academy', *Fast Capitalism*, 8(2) (www.uta.edu/huma/agger/fastcapitalism/8_2/Daniels8_2.html).

Daniels, J. and Gold, M. K. (2014) 'The InQ13 POOC: A participatory experiment in open, collaborative teaching and learning', *Journal of Interactive Technology & Pedagogy*, (5) (http://jitp.commons.gc.cuny.edu/the-inq13-pooc/).

Darnton, R. (2012) 'Digitize, democratize: Libraries and the future of books', *Columbia Journal of Law & the Arts*, 36(1), pp. 1–19.

Davidson, C. N. and Goldberg, D. T. (2010) *The future of thinking learning institutions in a digital age*. Cambridge, MA: The MIT Press (http://site.ebrary.com/id/10367819).

Dell, C. A., Low, C. and Wilker, J. F. (2010) 'Comparing student achievement in online and face-to-face class formats', *JOLT: Journal of Online Learning and Teaching*, 6(1), pp. 30–42.

DeMillo, R. A. (2015) *Revolution in higher education: How a small band of innovators will make college accessible and affordable*. Cambridge, MA: The MIT Press.

Devine, F., Friedman, S. and Newburn, T. (2013) *Social science in the public sphere: Riots, class and impact*. London School of Economics and Political Science (www.lse.ac.uk/newsAndMedia/videoAndAudio/channels/publicLecturesAndEvents/player.aspx?id=1948).

DOAJ (Directory of Open Access Journals) (2015) *Principles of transparency and best practice in scholarly publishing* (https://doaj.org/bestpractice).

DOER (Directory of Open Educational Resources) (2016) (http://doer.col.org/).

Doyle, C. (2013) 'Coursera and Chegg partner up to provide free textbooks for online courses', *Technapex*, May 8 (www.technapex. com/2013/05/coursera-and-chegg-partner-up-to-provide-free-textbooks-for-online-courses/).

Drabinski, E. (2014) 'Toward a kairos of library instruction', *The Journal of Academic Librarianship*, 40(5), pp. 480–5.

Edison Research (2015) 'The infinite dial 2015', *Edison Research*, March 4 (www.edisonresearch.com/the-infinite-dial-2015/).

Edlin, A. S. and Rubinfeld, D. L. (2004) 'Exclusive or efficient pricing? The big deal bundling of academic journals', *Antitrust Law Journal*, 72(1) (http://papers.ssrn.com/abstract=610103).

Educational Advisory Board (2010) *Maximizing space utilization: Measuring, allocating, and incentivizing efficient use of facilities*, *EAB Research and Insights Academic Affairs Forum* (www.eab.com/research-and-insights/academic-affairs-forum/studies/2010/maximizing-space-utilization).

Eligon, J. and Pérez-Peña, R. (2015) 'University of Missouri protests spur a day of change', *The New York Times*, November 9 (www. nytimes.com/2015/11/10/us/university-of-missouri-system-president-resigns.html).

Elsevier (2013) 'Elsevier to provide textbooks for five new edX MOOCs', October 23 (www.elsevier.com/about/press-releases/science-and-technology/elsevier-to-provide-textbooks-for-five-new-edx-moocs).

Eve, M. P. (2014) *Open access and the humanities: Contexts, controversies and the future*. Cambridge: Cambridge University Press (http://ebooks. cambridge.org/ebook.jsf?bid=CBO9781316161012).

Eysenbach, G. (2011) 'Can tweets predict citations? Metrics of social impact based on Twitter and correlation with traditional metrics of scientific impact', *Journal of Medical Internet Research*, 13(4), p. e123.

Fabricant, M. and Fine, M. (2012) *Charter schools and the corporate makeover of public education: What's at stake?* New York: Teachers College Press.

FemTechNet (2016) (http://femtechnet.org).

Fine, M. (2015) 'Global provocations: Critical reflections on community based research and intervention designed at the intersections of global dynamics and local cultures', *Community Psychology in Global Perspective*, 1(1).

Fister, B. (2016) *Creating an infrastructure for open access* (www. insidehighered.com/blogs/library-babel-fish/creating-infrastructure-open-access).

Fitzpatrick, K. (2010) 'Peer-to-peer review and the future of scholarly authority', *Social Epistemology*, 24(3), pp. 161–79.

Fitzpatrick, K. (2011) *Planned obsolescence: Publishing, technology, and the future of the academy*. New York: New York University Press.

Fitzpatrick, K. (2012) 'Openness, value, and scholarly societies: The Modern Language Association model', *College & Research Libraries News*, 73(11), pp. 650–3.

Fitzpatrick, K. (2015) 'Academia, not edu', *Planned Obsolescence*, October 26 (www.plannedobsolescence.net/academia-not-edu/).

Flaherty, C. (2015) 'Settling with Salaita', *Inside Higher Ed*, November 13 (www.insidehighered.com/news/2015/11/13/u-illinois-settles-professor-unhired-controversial-comments-twitter).

Folkenflik, D. (2012) 'MSNBC gets academic: Meet host Melissa Harris-Perry', *NPR*, July 20 (www.npr.org/2012/07/20/157070626/msnbc-gets-academic-effect-host-prof-harris-perry).

Fornthe, M. F., Shifflett, B. and Sibley, R. E. (2006) 'A comparison of online (high tech) and traditional (high touch) learning in business communication courses in Silicon Valley', *Journal of Education for Business*, 81(4), pp. 210–14.

Fowler, L. and Smith, K. (2013) 'Drawing the blueprint as we build: Setting up a library-based copyright and permissions service for MOOCs', *D-Lib Magazine*, 19 (7/8).

Freire, P. (1970) *Pedagogy of the oppressed*. New York: Herder & Herder.

Friedman, T. L. (2013) 'Revolution hits the universities', *The New York Times*, 27 January, p. 1(L).

Gardner, H. (2011) *The unschooled mind: How children think and how schools should teach*. New York: Basic Books.

Garfield, E. (1955) 'Citation indexes for science: A new dimension in documentation through association of ideas', *Science*, 122(3159), pp. 108–11.

Garfield, E. (2005) 'The agony and the ecstasy: The history and meaning of the journal impact factor', *International Congress on Peer Review and Biomedical Publication*, Chicago, IL (http://garfield.library.upenn.edu/papers/jifchicago2005.pdf).

Garfield, E. (2006) 'The history and meaning of the journal impact factor', *JAMA*, 295(1), pp. 90–3.

Garfield, E. and Malin, M. V. (1968) 'Can Nobel Prize winners be predicted?', *135th Annual Meeting, American Association for the Advancement of Science*, Dallas, TX (www.garfield.library.upenn.edu/papers/nobelpredicted.pdf).

Giddings, P. (2008) *Ida: A sword among lions: Ida B. Wells and the campaign against lynching*. New York: Amistad.

Giroux, H. (2008) *Against the terror of neoliberalism: Politics beyond the age of greed (Cultural politics and the promise of democracy)*. Boulder, CO: Paradigm Publishers.

Giroux, H. (2014) *Neoliberalism's war on higher education*. Chicago, IL: Haymarket Books.

Godin, S. (2010) 'The coming melt-down in higher education (as seen by a marketer)', April 29 (http://sethgodin.typepad.com/seths_blog/2010/04/the-coming-meltdown-in-higher-education-as-seen-by-a-marketer.html).

Gowers, T. (2012) 'Elsevier – my part in its downfall', *Gowers's Weblog: Mathematics related discussions*, January 21 (https://gowers.wordpress.com/2012/01/21/elsevier-my-part-in-its-downfall/).

Grasgreen, A. (2014) 'Options don't stem textbook woes' (www.insidehighered.com/news/2014/01/28/textbook-prices-still-crippling-students-report says).

Green, A. (2015) 'The financial calculations. Why Tim Wolfe had to resign', *The Atlantic*, November 9 (www.theatlantic.com/business/archive/2015/11/mizzou-tim-wolfe-resignation/414987/).

Gregory, K. (2013) 'The teaching of labor and the labor of teaching: Reflections on publicness and professionalism', *Journal of Interactive Technology & Pedagogy* (http://jitp.commons.gc.cuny.edu/the-teaching-of-labor-and-the-labor-of-teaching-reflections-on-publicness-and-professionalism/).

Grollman, E. A. (2015) 'Scholars under attack', *Inside Higher Ed* (www.insidehighered.com/advice/2015/07/09/essay-how-support-scholars-under-attack).

Gubrium, A. and Harper, K. (2013) *Participatory visual and digital methods*. Walnut Creek, CA: Left Coast Press.

Hamilton, A. (2015) 'San Francisco public library 1996', Ann Hamilton Studio (www.annhamiltonstudio.com/public/sanfrancisco.html).

Hargittai, I. (1999) 'Deeds and dreams of Eugene Garfield', *Chemical Intelligencer*, October, pp. 26–31.

Hawes, G. R. (1967) *To advance knowledge: A handbook on American university press publishing*. New York: Association of American University Presses.

Hazlett, C. (2014) 'Harvard and MIT release working papers on open online courses', *edX Blog*, January 21 (http://blog.edx.org/harvard-mit-release-working-papers-open/?track=blog).

Herbold, H. (1994) 'Never a level playing field: Blacks and the GI bill', *The Journal of Blacks in Higher Education*, (6), pp. 104–8.

Herman, T. and Banister, S. (2007) 'Face-to-face versus online coursework: A comparison of learning outcomes and costs', *Contemporary Issues in Technology and Teacher Education*, 7(4), pp. 318–26.

Hilton III, J. L. and Wiley, D. A. (2010) 'A sustainable future for open textbooks? The Flat World Knowledge story', *First Monday*, 15(8) (http://firstmonday.org/ojs/index.php/fm/article/view/2800).

Hinterberg, B. (2015) 'Community-engaged scholar award finalist Kristine Miller' [video], Minneapolis, MN: University of Minnesota (www.youtube.com/watch?v=EH_LkTghYg0).

Hoffer, T. B., Welch Jr., V. and National Opinion Research Center (2006) *Time to degree of US research doctorate recipients*. NSF06-312. National Science Foundation (www.nsf.gov/statistics/infbrief/nsf06312/nsf06312.pdf).

Holmwood, J. (2011) *A manifesto for the public university*. London: Bloomsbury Academic.

Holmwood, J. (2014) 'From social rights to the market: Neoliberalism and the knowledge economy', *International Journal of Lifelong Education*, 33(1), pp. 62–76.

Hoole, S. R. H. (2014) 'Gaming the system: Manipulating the impact factor in research', *IEEE Roundup*, September 25 (http://theinstitute.ieee.org/ieee-roundup/opinions/ieee-roundup/gaming-the-system-manipulating-the-impact-factor-in-research).

Howard, D. L. (2014) 'A teaching career in fragments', *The Chronicle of Higher Education*, February 24 (http://chronicle.com/article/A-Teaching-Career-in-Fragments/144911).

Howard, J. (2013) 'For libraries, MOOCs bring uncertainty and opportunity', *Wired Campus*, March 25 (http://chronicle.com/blogs/wiredcampus/for-libraries-moocs-bring-uncertainty-and-opportunity/43111).

Hynes, E. (2012) 'We're living in a golden age of documentary filmmaking', *Slate*, February 14 (www.slate.com/articles/arts/culturebox/2012/02/tabloid_senna_the_interrupters_and_other_documentaries_overlooked_by_the_academy.html).

Izadi, E. (2015) 'The incidents that led to the University of Missouri president's resignation', *The Washington Post*, November 9 (www.washingtonpost.com/news/grade-point/wp/2015/11/09/the-incidents-that-led-to-the-university-of-missouri-presidents-resignation/).

Jacoby, R. (1987) *The last intellectuals: American culture in the age of academe*. New York: Basic Books.

Jarecki, E. (2013) 'The house I live in'. New York: Virgil Films.

Jasco, P. (2010) 'The impact of Eugene Garfield through the prism of Web of Science', *Annals of Library and Information Studies*, 57, pp. 222–47.

Jha, A. (2012) 'Academic spring: how an angry maths blog sparked a scientific revolution', *The Guardian*, April 9 (www.theguardian. com/science/2012/apr/09/frustrated-blogpost-boycott-scientific-journals).

Jiménez, A. C., Boyer, D., Hartigan, J. and de la Cadena, M. (2015) *Open access: A collective ecology for AAA publishing in the digital age – Cultural anthropology* (www.culanth.org/fieldsights/684-open-access-a-collective-ecology-for-aaa-publishing-in-the-digital-age).

Johnson, J. (2013) 'Using Twitter for curated academic content', *Impact of Social Sciences*, January 18 (http://blogs.lse.ac.uk/impactofsocialsciences/2013/01/18/using-twitter-for-curated-academic-content/).

Johnson, S. (1997) *Interface culture: How new technology transforms the way we create and communicate.* San Francisco, CA: HarperEdge.

Jones, S., and Mauer, M. (2013) *Race to incarcerate: A graphic retelling.* New York: The New Press.

Jurgenson, N. (2012) 'The IRL fetish', *The New Inquiry* (http://thenewinquiry.com/essays/the-irl-fetish/).

JustPublics@365 (2013a) *Imagining New York City after stop-and-frisk.* Pressbooks (https://archive.org/details/JP365-NYCAfterStopAndFriskModulePacket2013FINAL2[archive.org).

JustPublics@365 (2013b) *JustPublics@365 Toolkit: A social media guide for academics.* New York (http://justpublics365.commons.gc.cuny. edu/files/2013/12/JustPublics365_Toolkit.pdf).

JustPublics@365 (2014a) 'MediaCamp participant survey data report January-December 2013' (http://justpublics365.commons.gc.cuny. edu/files/2015/03/JP365_MediaCampReport_2013-14.pdf).

JustPublics@365 (2014b) 'Podcasts' (http://justpublics365.commons. gc.cuny.edu/podcasts/).

JustPublics@365 (2016) Archive-It CUNY Research Projects Web Archive (CUNY Graduate Center) (http://wayback.archive-it. org/5484/*/http://justpublics365.commons.gc.cuny.edu/).

Karaganis, J. and McClure, D. (2016) 'What a million syllabuses can teach us', *The New York Times*, January 22 (www.nytimes. com/2016/01/24/opinion/sunday/what-a-million-syllabuses-can-teach-us.html).

Karpf, D. (2010) 'Online political mobilization from the advocacy group's perspective: Looking beyond clicktivism', *Policy & Internet*, 2(4), pp. 7–41.

Kendrick, C. and Gashurov, I. (2013) 'Libraries in the time of MOOCs', *Educause review online*, November 4 (www.educause.edu/ero/article/libraries-time-moocs).

Kendzior, S. (2014) 'The adjunct crisis is everyone's problem', Vitae, October 17 (https://chroniclevitae.com/news/762-the-adjunct-crisis-is-everyone-s-problem).

Kennison, R. and Norberg, L. (2014) *A scalable and sustainable approach to open access publishing and archiving for humanities and social sciences* (http://knconsultants.org/toward-a-sustainable-approach-to-open-access-publishing-and-archiving/).

Khamis, S. and Vaughn, K. (2012) '"We are all Khaled Said": The potentials and limitations of cyberactivism in triggering public mobilization and promoting political change', *Journal of Arab & Muslim Media Research*, 4(2-3), pp. 145–163.

King, A. (1993) 'From sage on the stage to guide on the side', *College Teaching*, 41(1), pp. 30–5.

King, S. (2015) 'Pink ribbons, Inc.' Email correspondence with J. Daniels.

Kingsley, D. and Harnad, S. (2015) 'Dutch universities plan Elsevier boycott – will this be a game changer or will publisher profits remain unaffected?', *Impact of Social Sciences*, London School of Economics, July 8 (http://blogs.lse.ac.uk/impactofsocialsciences/2015/07/08/dutch-universities-boycott-elsevier/).

Klocker, N. and Drozdzewski, D. (2012) 'Commentary: Career progress relative to opportunity: How many papers is a baby "worth"?', *Environment and Planning A*, 44(6), pp. 1271–7.

K|N Consultants (2016) 'Be informed.' Open Access Network (http://openaccessnetwork.org/be-informed).

Knoblauch, H. (2014) 'JustPublics@365 interview with documentary filmmaker Dawn Porter', February 28 (https://justpublics365.commons.gc.cuny.edu/2014/02/28/special-interview-documentary-filmmaker-dawn-porter/ and https://archive.org/details/JP365-DocumentaryFilmSeriesDawnPorterOnGideonsArmy[archive.org]).

Koory, M. A. (2003) 'Differences in learning outcomes for the online and f2f versions of "An Introduction to Shakespeare"', *Journal of Asynchronous Learning Networks*, 7(2), pp. 18–35.

Kraft, T. (2013) 'Adjunctification: Living in the margins of academe', *Hybrid Pedagogy* (www.hybridpedagogy.com/journal/adjunctification-living-in-the-margins-of-academe/).

Kristof, N. (2014a) 'Bridging the moat around universities', *New York Times: The Opinion Pages: On the Ground*, February 15 (http://kristof.blogs.nytimes.com/2014/02/15/bridging-the-moat-around-universities/).

Kristof, N. (2014b) 'Professors, we need you!', *The New York Times*, February 15 (www.nytimes.com/2014/02/16/opinion/sunday/kristof-professors-we-need-you.html).

Kryllidou, M., Morris, S. and Robuck, G. (2012) 'Monograph and serial costs in ARL libraries, 1986-2011', in *ARL Statistics 2010-2011*. Washington, DC: Association of Research Libraries (http://publications.arl.org/ARL-Statistics-2010-2011).

Ladson-Billings, G. (2006) 'From the achievement gap to the education debt: Understanding achievement in US schools', *Educational Researcher*, 35(7), pp. 3–12.

Lamont, M. (2009) *How professors think: Inside the curious world of academic judgment*. Cambridge, MA: Harvard University Press.

Lamont, M. (2012) 'Toward a comparative sociology of valuation and evaluation', *Annual Review of Sociology*, 38(1), pp. 201–21.

Lamont, M. and Huutoniemi, K. (2011) 'Opening the black box of evaluation: How quality is recognized by peer review panels', *Bulletin SAGW*, 2, pp. 47–9.

Lane, P. (1992) 'Thomson corporation acquires majority interest in ISI', *Information Today* (www.highbeam.com/doc/1G1-12296761.html).

Larivière, V., Haustein, S. and Mongeon, P. (2015) 'The oligopoly of academic publishers in the digital era', *PLOS ONE*, 10(6), p. e0127502.

Larson, S. (2015) '"Invisibilia" and the evolving art of radio', *The New Yorker*, January 21 (www.newyorker.com/culture/sarah-larson/invisibilia-evolving-art-radio).

Leiner, B., Cerf, V., Clark, D., Kahn, R., Kleinrock, L., Lynch, D. Postel, J., Roberts, L.G. and Wolff, S. (2012) *Brief history of the Internet*. Internet Society (www.internetsociety.org/brief-history-internet).

Lepore, J. (2013) 'The new economy of letters', *The Chronicle of Higher Education*, September 3 (http://chronicle.com/article/The-New-Economy-of-Letters/141291/).

Lewin, T. (2013) 'Gap widens for faculty at colleges, report finds', *The New York Times*, April 8 (www.nytimes.com/2013/04/08/education/gap-in-university-faculty-pay-continues-to-grow-report-finds.html)

Lewis, D. L. (2000) *W.E.B. DuBois: The fight for equality and the American century, 1919-1963*. New York: H. Holt.

Löfgren, O. (2014) 'Routinising research: Academic skills in analogue and digital worlds', *International Journal of Social Research Methodology*, 17(1), pp. 73–86.

Losh, E. (ed.) (2016) *The MOOC moment: Experiments in scale and access in higher education*. Chicago, IL: University of Chicago Press.

Lupton, D. (2014) *Digital sociology*. New York: Routledge.

Marcus, J. (2014) 'New analysis shows problematic boom in higher ed administrators', *The Huffington Post* (www.huffingtonpost.com/2014/02/06/higher-ed-administrators-growth_n_4738584.html).

Matthew, P. A. (2016) *Written/unwritten: Diversity and the hidden truths of tenure.* Chapel Hill, NC: University of North Carolina Press.

Matthews, D. (2015) 'Altmetrics risk becoming part of problem, not solution, warns academic', *Times Higher Education (THE)*, October 7 (www.timeshighereducation.com/news/altmetrics-risk-becoming-part-problem-not-solution-warns-academic).

Mauer, M. and Sentencing Project (1999) *Race to incarcerate.* New York: New Press.

McFadden, S. (2014) 'What Nicholas Kristof gets wrong about public intellectuals', *Feministing*, February (http://feministing.com/2014/02/19/what-nicholas-kristof-gets-wrong-about-public-intellectuals/).

McKenna, L. (2015) 'The convoluted profits of academic publishing', *The Atlantic*, December 17 (www.theatlantic.com/education/archive/2015/12/the-convoluted-profits-of-academic-publishing/421047/).

Means, B., Toyama, Y., Murphy, R., Bakia, M. and Jones, K. (2010) *Evaluation of evidence-based practices in online learning: a meta-analysis and review of online learning studies.* Washington, DC: US Department of Education, Office of Planning, Evaluation, and Policy Development, Policy and Program Studies Service Center for Technology in Learning (www2.ed.gov/rschstat/eval/tech/evidence-based-practices/finalreport.pdf).

Mills, C. W. (1959) *The sociological imagination.* New York: Oxford University Press.

Moody, G. (2015) 'Entire editorial staff of Elsevier journal *Lingua* resigns over high price, lack of open access', *Ars Technica UK* (http://arstechnica.co.uk/science/2015/11/entire-editorial-staff-of-elsevier-journal-lingua-resigns-over-high-price-lack-of-open-access/).

Morris, A. D. (2015) *The scholar denied: W.E.B. DuBois and the birth of modern sociology.* Oakland, CA: University of California Press

Mortenson, T. (2012) 'State funding: A race to the bottom', *American Council on Education* (www.acenet.edu/the-presidency/columns-and-features/Pages/state-funding-a-race-to-the-bottom.aspx).

Mundy, L. (2014) 'The media has a woman problem', *The New York Times*, April 26 (www.nytimes.com/2014/04/27/opinion/sunday/the-media-has-a-woman-problem.html).

Newburn, T. (2015) 'The 2011 England riots in recent historical perspective', *British Journal of Criminology*, 55(1), pp. 39–64.

New York Times, The (2013) Editorial Board: 'The next step in drug treatment', 27 April, p. A20(L).

Neylon, T. (2012) *The cost of knowledge* (http://thecostofknowledge. com/).

Noguera, P. (2003) *City schools and the American dream: Reclaiming the promise of public education*. New York: Teachers College Press.

O'Reilly, T. (2004) 'The architecture of participation', *O'Reilly*, June (http://archive.oreilly.com/pub/a/oreilly/tim/articles/architecture_ of_participation.html).

OA Community (2016) *Journal declarations of independence, Open Access Directory* (http://oad.simmons.edu/oadwiki/Journal_declarations_ of_independence).

Oakerson, A. and O'Donnell, J. (1995) *Scholarly journals at the crossroads: A subversive proposal for electronic publishing*. Washington, DC: Association of Research Libraries (http://hdl.handle.net/2027/ mdp.39015034923758).

Onink, T. (2013) 'Georgia Tech, Udacity shock higher ed with $7,000 degree', *Forbes* (www.forbes.com/sites/troyonink/2013/05/15/ georgia-tech-udacity-shock-higher-ed-with-7000- degree/#18a3352a7e89).

Otani, A. (2015) 'Student groups pressure colleges over the insane cost of textbooks', *Bloomberg.com* (www.bloomberg.com/news/ articles/2015-02-27/student-groups-pressure-colleges-over-the- insane-cost-of-textbooks).

Otte, G. (2012) 'Degrees of openness?', *Tributaries: occasional affluents to the confluence*, November 12 (http://purelyreactive.commons.gc.cuny. edu/2012/11/12/degrees-of-openness/).

Pappano, L. (2012) 'The year of the MOOC', *The New York Times*, November 4, p. 26(L).

Parr, C. (2014) 'Imperial College London to "review procedures" after death of academic', *Times Higher Education (THE)* (www. timeshighereducation.com/news/imperial-college-london-to- review-procedures-after-death-of-academic/2017188.article).

Pearson, C. (2014) 'Why I (stupidly?) took Nick Kristof's clickbait personally – or, where #EngagedAcademics came from', *Another fine mess*, February 15 (https://chuckpearson.wordpress. com/2014/02/15/why-i-stupidly-took-nick-kristofs-clickbait- personally-or-where-engagedacademics-came-from/).

Picciano, A. G. (2002) 'Beyond student perceptions: Issues of interaction, presence, and performance in an online course', *Journal of Asynchronous Learning Networks*, 6(1), pp. 21–40.

Picciano, A. G. (2014) 'MOOCs: The hype, the backlash, and the future!', *University Outlook*, 1(4) (http://anthonypicciano.com/pdfs/Hype-Backlash-Future.pdf).

Piven, F. F. (2013) 'Frances Fox Piven on the development of the welfare state, voting, and activism in the academy' (http://justpublics365.commons.gc.cuny.edu/2013/11/04/frances-fox-piven-development-welfare-state-voting-activism-academy/).

Priem, J., Piwowar, H.A. and Hemminger, B.M. (2012) 'Altmetrics in the wild: Using social media to explore scholarly impact', arXiv:1203.4745v1.

Priem, J., Taraborelli, D., Groth, P. and Neylon, C. (2010) *Altmetrics: A manifesto*. October 26 (http://altmetrics.org/manifesto/).

Pugh, T., Netherland, J. and Finkelstein, R. (2013) *Blueprint for a public health and safety approach to drug policy*. New York Academy of Medicine and the Drug Policy Alliance (www.drugpolicy.org/sites/default/files/3371_DPA_NYAM_Report_FINAL_for_WEB%20April%2019%202013.pdf).

Queens Library (2014) 'An interview with author and historian Jelani Cobb', *Queens Library*, December 29 (www.queenslibrary.org/blog/an-interview-with-author-historian-jelani-cobb).

Reading the Riots (2012) 'Court order prevents BBC from broadcasting film about riots', *The Guardian*, July 19 (www.theguardian.com/uk/series/reading-the-riots).

Rey, P.J. (2012) 'The myth of cyberspace', *The New Inquiry*, April 13 (http://thenewinquiry.com/essays/the-myth-of-cyberspace/).

Ritzer, G. and Jurgenson, N. (2010) 'Production, consumption, prosumption: The nature of capitalism in the age of the digital "prosumer"', *Journal of Consumer Culture*, 10(1), pp. 13–36.

Rivard, R. (2013) 'Citing disappointing student outcomes, San Jose State pauses work with Udacity project on pause', July 18 (www.insidehighered.com/news/2013/07/18/citing-disappointing-student-outcomes-san-jose-state-pauses-work-udacity).

Roose, K. (2014) 'What's behind the great podcast renaissance?', *New York Magazine Daily Intelligencer*, October 30 (http://nymag.com/daily/intelligencer/2014/10/whats-behind-the-great-podcast-renaissance.html).

Sabaratnam, M. and Kirby, P. (2014) 'Why metrics cannot measure research quality: a response to the HEFCE consultation', *The Disorder of Things*, June 16 (http://thedisorderofthings.com/2014/06/16/why-metrics-cannot-measure-research-quality-a-response-to-the-hefce-consultation/).

Saltmarsh, J. and Hartley, M. (2011) *To serve a larger purpose: Engagement for democracy and the transformation of higher education.* Philadelphia, PA: Temple University Press.

Sample, I. (2012) 'Harvard University says it can't afford journal publishers' prices', *The Guardian*, April 24 (www.theguardian.com/science/2012/apr/24/harvard-university-journal-publishers-prices).

Samson, N. (2015) 'A behind-the-scenes look at the mass resignations at Lingua', *University Affairs*, November 24 (www.universityaffairs.ca/news/news-article/a-behind-the-scenes-look-at-the-mass-resignations-at-lingua).

Sassen, S. (2002) 'Towards a sociology of information technology', *Current Sociology*, 50(3), pp. 365-88.

Savio, M. (1964) 'Sit-in address on the steps of Sproul Hall', Berkeley, CA, December 2 (www.americanrhetoric.com/speeches/mariosaviosproulhallsitin.htm).

Schuman, R. (2015) 'The humiliating nightmare of academic-conference season', *Slate*, December 9 (www.slate.com/articles/life/education/2015/12/the_humiliating_nightmare_of_academic_conference_season.html).

Scudellari, M. (2010) 'Library cuts threaten research', *The Scientist* (www.the-scientist.com/?articles.view/articleNo/29291/title/Library-cuts-threaten-research/).

Seale, M. (2010) 'Information literacy standards and the politics of knowledge production: Using user-generated content to incorporate critical pedagogy', in M.T. Accardi, E. Drabinski and A. Kumbier (eds) *Critical library instruction: Theories and methods.* Duluth, MN: Library Juice Press, pp. 221–35.

Shenk, D. (1997) *Data smog: surviving the information glut.* San Francisco, CA: Harper Edge.

SHERPA/RoMEO (2016) *RoMEO statistics* (www.sherpa.ac.uk/romeo/statistics.php?la=en&fIDnum=|&mode=simple).

Shieber, S. (2013) 'Why open access is better for scholarly societies', *The Occasional Pamphlet*, January 29 (https://blogs.harvard.edu/pamphlet/2013/01/29/why-open-access-is-better-for-scholarly-societies/).

Shor, I. and Freire, P. (2003) 'What are the fears and risks of transformation?', in A. Darder, M. Baltodano and R. D. Torres (eds) *The Critical Pedagogy Reader*. New York: RoutledgeFalmer, pp. 479–96.

Shore, C. and Wright, S. (2000) 'Coercive accountability: The rise of audit culture in higher education', in M. Strathern (ed.) *Audit cultures: Anthropological studies in accountability, ethics and the academy*. New York: Routledge.

Shulenburger, D. E. (1999) 'Moving with dispatch to resolve the scholarly communication crisis: From here to near', *ARL: A bimonthly report*, (202), pp. 2–3.

Small, H. (2007) 'Eugene Garfield, scientist' (www.webofstories.com/play/eugene.garfield/1.

Smith, K. (2013) 'A discouraging day in court for GSU', *Scholarly Communications @ Duke*, November 20 (http://blogs.library.duke.edu/scholcomm/2013/11/20/a-discouraging-day-in-court-for-gsu/).

Smith-Cruz, S., Thistlethwaite, P. and Daniels, J. (2014) 'Open scholarship for open education: Building the JustPublics@365 POOC', *Journal of Library Innovation*, 5(2), pp. 15–28.

Starkman, R. (2013) 'What "counts"?', *Inside Higher Ed*, February 20 (www.insidehighered.com/advice/2013/02/20/essay-issues-related-what-digital-scholarship-counts-tenure-and-promotion).

Stein, A. and Daniels, J. (2017) *Going public: A guide for social scientists*. Chicago, IL: University of Chicago Press.

Stewart, B. E. (2013) 'Massiveness + openness = new literacies of participation?', *JOLT: Journal of Online Learning and Teaching*, 9(2) (http://jolt.merlot.org/vol9no2/stewart_bonnie_0613.htm).

Stewart, B. E. (2015) 'In abundance: Networked participatory practices as scholarship', *The International Review of Research in Open and Distributed Learning*, 16(3), pp. 318–40.

Stommel, J. (2012) 'Online learning: a manifesto', *Hybrid Pedagogy* (www.hybridpedagogy.com/journal/online-learning-a-manifesto/).

Stoudt, B. G. and Torre, M. E. (2014) 'The Morris Justice Project: Participatory Action Research', *SAGE Research Methods*. London: Sage Publications (http://srmo.sagepub.com/view/methods-case-studies-2014/n379.xml).

Stoudt, B. G. and Torre, M. E. (2015) 'The Morris Justice Project.' In P. Brindle (ed) *SAGE cases in methodology*. London: Sage.

Stoudt, B. G., Fox, M. and Fine, M. (2012) 'Contesting privilege with critical participatory action research', *Journal of Social Issues*, 68(1), pp. 178–93.

Stoudt, B. G., Torre, M. E., Bartley, P., Bracy, F., Caldwell, H., Downs, A. et al (2015) '"This is OUR home": The Morris Justice Project, participatory action research and our pursuit of public policy change.' In C. Durose and L. Richardson (eds) *Designing public policy for co-production.* Bristol: Policy Press.

Straumshein, C. (2016) 'The limits of open', *Inside Higher Ed*, January 29 (www.insidehighered.com/news/2016/01/29/critics-see-mismatch-between-courseras-mission-business-model).

Strauss, V. (2016) 'More US academic groups join boycott of Israel – and critics push back', *The Washington Post*, January 18 (www.washingtonpost.com/news/answer-sheet/wp/2016/01/18/more-u-s-academic-groups-join-boycott-of-israel-and-critics-push-back/).

Street, S., Maisto, M., Merves, E. and Rhoades, G. (2012) *Who is Professor "Staff," and how can this person teach so many classes?* Center for the Future of Higher Education (www.nfmfoundation.org/ProfStaffFinal.pdf).

Suber, P. (2012) *Open access.* Cambridge, MA: The MIT Press (https://mitpress.mit.edu/index.php?q=books/open-access).

Supiano, B. (2015) 'Racial disparities in higher education: An overview', *The Chronicle of Higher Education*, November 10 (http://chronicle.com/article/Racial-Disparities-in-Higher/234129).

Tadween Editors (2013) 'Interview: Sarah Kendzior on open access in academia', Tadween Publishing (http://tadweenpublishing.com/blogs/news/9652021-interview-sarah-kendzior-on-open-access-in-academia).

Tallent-Runnels, M. K., Thomas, J. A., Lan, W. Y., Cooper, S., Ahern, T. C., Shaw, S. M. and Liu, X. (2006) 'Teaching courses online: A review of the research', *Review of Educational Research*, 76(1), pp. 93–135.

Tamburri, R. (2014) 'An interview with Canadian MOOC pioneer George Siemens', *University Affairs*, February 12 (www.universityaffairs.ca/features/feature-article/an-interview-with-canadian-mooc-pioneer-george-siemens/).

Terras, M. (2012) 'The verdict: is blogging or tweeting about research papers worth it?', *Impact of Social Sciences*, April 19 (http://blogs.lse.ac.uk/impactofsocialsciences/2012/04/19/blog-tweeting-papers-worth-it/).

THE (*Times Higher Education*) (2001) 'Outbreak of "new managerialism" infects faculties', July 20 (www.timeshighereducation.com/news/outbreak-of-new-managerialism-infects-faculties/164003.article).

The Economist (2011) 'Of goats and headaches', May 26 (www.economist.com/node/18744177).

The Illuminator (2012) 'Stop and frisk in the South Bronx' (www.youtube.com/watch?v=mliuISC2hJk).

'The Illuminator' (no date) (http://theilluminator.org/).

The VozMob Project (2011) 'Mobile voices: Projecting the voices of immigrant workers by appropriating mobile phones for popular communication', in *Communications Research in Action: Scholar-Activist Collaborations for a Democratic Public Sphere*. NY: Fordham University Press, pp. 177–96.

Thomson, P. (2014) 'academics all write badly... another response to a familiar critique', *patter*, February 17 (http://patthomson.net/2014/02/17/academics-all-write-badly/).

Toral, A. (2014) *JustPublics@365: MediaCamp workshops*. New York (https://vimeo.com/79754862).

Torre, M. E., Stoudt, B. G., Manoff, E. and Fine, M. (2016) 'Critical participatory action research: Inquiry designed in fragile solidarities.' In N. Denzin and Y. S. Lincoln (eds) *Handbook of qualitative research* (5th edn) London: Sage Publications.

Tufekci, Z. (2015) 'Facebook said its algorithms do help form echo chambers, and the tech press missed it', *New Perspectives Quarterly*, 32(3), pp. 9–12.

Udell, J. (2012). 'A domain of one's own', *Wired*, July 27 (www.wired.com/insights/2012/07/a-domain-of-ones-own/).

Umbach, P. D. and Wawrzynski, M. R. (2005) 'Faculty do matter: The role of college faculty in student learning and engagement', *Research in Higher Education*, 46(2), pp. 153–84.

Vaidhyanathan, S. (2011) *The Googlization of everything (and why we should worry)*. Berkeley, CA: University of California Press.

van Noorden, R. (2014) 'Google Scholar pioneer on search engine's future', *Nature*. doi: 10.1038/nature.2014.16269.

Vanclay, J. (2008) 'Bias in the journal impact factor', *Scientometrics*, 78(1), pp. 3–12. Veletsianos, G. and Kimmons, R. (2012) 'Assumptions and challenges of open scholarship', *The International Review of Research in Open and Distributed Learning*, 13(4), pp. 166–89.

Voeten, E. (2014) 'Dear Nicholas Kristof: we are right here!', *The Washington Post, Monkey Cage*, February 15 (www.washingtonpost.com/news/monkey-cage/wp/2014/02/15/dear-nicholas-kristof-we-are-right-here/).

Wade, L. (2015) 'Lisa Wade'. Telephone interview with J. Daniels, September 4.

Wade, L. and Sharp, G. (2013) 'Sociological images blogging as public sociology', *Social Science Computer Review*, 31(2), pp. 221–8. Wajcman, J. (2002) 'Addressing technological change: The challenge to social theory', *Current sociology*, 50(3), pp 347–63.

Warren, L. L. and Holloman, H. L. (2005) 'Online instruction: Are the outcomes the same?', *Journal of Instructional Psychology*, 32(2), p. 148.

Waters, J. K. (2013) 'What will happen to MOOCs now that Udacity is leaving higher ed?', *Campus Technology*, December 11 (https://campustechnology.com/Articles/2013/12/11/What-Will-Happen-to-MOOCs-Now-that-Udacity-Is-Leaving-Higher-Ed.aspx).

Watters, A. (2013) 'Coursera, Chegg, and the education enclosure movement', *Hack Education*, May 8 (http://hackeducation.com/2013/05/08/coursera-chegg/).

Watters, A. (2015) 'The MOOC revolution that wasn't', *The Kernel*, August 23 (http://kernelmag.dailydot.com/issue-sections/headline-story/14046/mooc-revolution-uber-for-education/).

Weber, J. M. and Lennon, R. (2007) 'Multi-course comparison of traditional versus web-based course delivery systems', *Journal of Educators Online*, 4(2), pp. 1–19.

Weller, M. (2011) *The digital scholar: How technology is transforming scholarly practice*. London: Bloomsbury Publishing PLC (www.bloomsburycollections.com/book/the-digital-scholar-how-technology-is-transforming-scholarly-practice/).

Wente, M. (2014) 'How women are losing the pundit war', *The Globe and Mail*, May 24 (www.theglobeandmail.com/opinion/how-women-are-losing-the-pundit-war/article18812139/).

Westerling, K. (2016) 'Self-evaluating a first semester of technologically teaching speech', *The Futures Initiative*, January 15 (http://futures.gc.cuny.edu/blog/2016/01/15/self-evaluating-a-first-semester-of-technologically-teaching-speech/).

Wilder, C. S. (2013) *Ebony and ivy: Race, slavery, and the troubled history of America's universities*. New York: Bloomsbury Press.

Willinsky, J. (2004) 'Scholarly associations and the economic viability of open access publishing', *Journal of Digital Information*, 4(2) (https://journals.tdl.org/jodi/index.php/jodi/article/view/104).

Wilsdon, J., Allen, L., Belfiore, E., Campbell, P., Curry, S., Hill, S. Jones, R., Hill, J., Kain, R., Johnson, B., Kerridge, S., Tinkler, J., Thelwall, M., Wouters, P. and Viney, I. (2015) *The metric tide: Report of the independent review of the role of metrics in research assessment and management*. Higher Education Funding Council for England (www.hefce.ac.uk/pubs/rereports/Year/2015/metrictide/Title,104463,en.html).

Wilson, J. (2015) 'How Black Lives Matter saved higher education', *Al Jazeera America* (http://america.aljazeera.com/opinions/2015/12/how-black-lives-matter-saved-higher-education.html).

Wise, A., Chang, J., Duffy, T. and Valle, R. D. (2004) 'The effects of teacher social presence on student satisfaction, engagement, and learning', *Journal of Educational Computing Research*, 31(3), pp. 247–71

Woodhouse, K. (2015) 'Who's to blame for rising tuition?, *Inside Higher Ed*. May 5 (www.insidehighered.com/news/2015/05/05/report-says-administrative-bloat-construction-booms-not-largely-responsible-tuition).

Xin, X. (2010) 'The impact of "citizen journalism" on Chinese media and society', *Journalism Practice*, 4(3), pp. 333–44.

Zickuhr, K. and Rainie, L. (2014) 'E-reading rises as device ownership jumps', *Pew Research Center: Internet, Science & Tech*, January 16 (www.pewinternet.org/2014/01/16/e-reading rises-as-device-ownership-jumps/).

Index

Page references for notes are followed by n

A

Academia.edu 72, 76
academic conferences 12–13, 31–3,
    34, 35–7
academic publishing *see* scholarly
    publishing
Academic Spring 67
academics
  as authors 61–2, 67, 90
  digital media skills 89–107, 133–4
  public engagement 89–90, 92–4,
    103–4, 105–7
  scholarly societies and associations
    67–8
  structure of habits 9–14
  tenure and contingency 14–15
  see also impact
access *see* open access
Acharya, Anurag 110–11
ACT UP 59–60, 79–80
activism
  ACT UP 59–60
  Twitter 98–9
  see also scholar-activism
Addiction Series, The 27
African Americans 24, 127–8
African Journals Online 73
AIDS 59–60
Alperin, Juan Pablo 121
altmetrics 31, 119–21, 124, 134
alumni 63
American Anthropological
    Association 70, 85

American Association of University
    Professors (AAUP) 14
American Sociological Association
    106–7
analytics 100
Antipode Foundation 22
Arts and Humanities Citation Index
    (AHCI) 112
Association of Research Libraries 66
AT&T 46
audit culture 115
authors 61–2, 67, 90
  copyright 3, 62, 80, 84, 138
  publishing charges 69, 73–4
  self-archiving 75–7, 82, 84, 87
  textbooks 71
Authors Alliance 138

B

Bady, Aaron 41, 43, 48
Balsamo, Anne 55
Basel 56
Battle, Juan 35
Bergstrom, T. C. 65
bibliometrics 112, 116
big data 25, 32, 79
BioMed Central 60, 73, 74
#BlackLivesMatter 127, 129
blogs 6, 92–3, 99–100, 106
  blog-to-book 2, 3, 33–4
*Blueprint for a public health and safety
    approach to drug policy* 32
Bookchin, Natalie 31

books 11, 19
  blog-to-book 2, 3, 33–4
  open access 3, 8, 78–9
  textbooks 71, 85
  university presses 70–1
  see also eBooks
Bowen, William G. 44–5
boyd, danah 78–9
Boyer, Ernest 29–30, 56, 109–10,
  111, 116, 120, 121, 126–7, 128,
  129
Brazil 73
Bronx 22–3
Brown, Michael 24, 98, 127
Buckingham, Robert 66
Butler, Jonathan 127, 134
Butler, Octavia 2, 131, 132, 135, 139

C

Cahill, Caitlin 82
Cambridge University Press vs Patton
  51–2, 57n
Campbell, L. 22
Canadian Institute of Health 74
card catalogs 132–3
Carnegie Classifications of
  Institutions of Higher Education
  78
Carrigan, Mark 9–10, 81, 102
Chegg 43
Chin, Margaret 35
Chuang, Isaac 55–6
citation analysis 112–14, 117, 119,
  122, 124
citation management 2, 11–12
citizen journalism 25
City University of New York
  (CUNY) 18, 48
  digital media training 90–1, 133
  #InQ13 48–54
  MediaCamp 94–100, 103, 105
  metrics survey 125–6
  see also JustPublics@365
classroom management 5
clicktivism 23
Coates, Ta-Nehisi 1, 29
Cobb, Jelani 24, 29
coercive citations 113
collaboration 2, 6, 12, 13–14, 24
  citation management 11–12
  with journalism and documentary
  filmmaking 24–37, 133

College Board 71
Commentpress 3
commercialization 8–9, 17, 43,
  47–8, 137–9
Commonwealth of Learning 81
communities, engagement with
  universities 22–3, 48–51, 53–6,
  123–4, 136–7
Concerned Student 1-9-5-0 127
conferences 12–13, 31–3, 34, 35–7
content management systems 3, 92
continuous publishing 10, 81, 85
Conversation, The 92
copyright 3, 62, 80, 84, 138
  course readings 51–2, 57n
Cormier, Dave 41, 136
cost disease 44, 45, 135
Cost of Knowledge, The 67
Cottom, Tressie McMillan 41, 102
Coursera 40, 43, 52
Crisis, The 21, 37
Cultural Anthropology 64, 70, 79, 85,
  137
curricula 42

D

Darnton, Robert 7, 8–9, 13, 136
Data & Society 79
data visualization 25, 32
Davidson, Cathy N. 8
Declaration on Research Assessment
  (DORA) 114
DeMillo, Richard 45–8, 116
democratization 8–9, 17, 55–6, 86,
  137
Detroit 22, 23
digital media technologies 1
  measuring impact 110–11, 118–26
  personal experience 6–7
  training 89–107, 133–4
  see also Internet, eBooks
digital scholarship 1–2
  commercialization and
  democratization 8–9, 17–18
  and documentary filmmaking 24,
  27–9, 31–7
  future 131–9
  and journalism 24–7, 29–37
  JustPublics@365 18–19
  and open access 71–9
  personal experience 6–7
  reimagining communication 29–37

scholar-activism 22–3
scholarship of engagement 109–10
and structure of habits 9–14
transforming scholarly life 2–6
Din, Ravida 28
Directory of Open Access Journals
(DOAJ) 73, 84, 86
dissertations 7
distributed open collaborative courses
(DOCCs) 55, 136
doctoral training 90–1
documentary filmmaking 22, 24,
27–9, 31–7, 133
open access 83–4
Dorner, Jennifer 52
Drug Policy Alliance (DPA) 32
DuBois, W. E. B. 4, 21, 24, 37
Duggan, Mark 23

E

e-reserves case 51–2, 57n
East Harlem 48–54, 82–3, 102–3
eBooks 11, 35, 36–7
open access 81–2, 85
social justice series 33–4
education *see* higher education
Education Reform Act 1988 115
Educational Advisory Board 16
edX 43, 52
Elsevier 43, 63, 64, 68
and Academia.edu 72, 76
boycott 67
hybrid publishing models 73
and *Lingua* 69
engagement 89–90, 92–4, 103–4,
105–7
with communities 22–3, 48–51,
53–6, 123–4, 136–7
Open Syllabus Project 122–3
scholarship of engagement 109–10,
120, 121, 126–7, 129, 134
European Research Council 74

F

Facebook 93, 98–9
faculty *see* academics
Farkas, Susan 95–6
FemTechNet 13, 55
Ferguson, Missouri 24, 98, 127
Fernandes, Sujatha 94, 95, 96, 101

filmmaking *see* documentary
filmmaking
Fister, Barbara 77, 78
Fitzpatrick, Kathleen 3, 4, 72, 120–1
Floyd et al vs City of New York 2013
34
Friedman, Thomas 15, 39

G

Garageband 98
Garfield, Eugene 111–14, 116,
117–19, 121, 134
Gashurov, I. 52
Georgia State University 51–2, 57n
Georgia Tech University 46, 56n
GI Bill 128
Gillen, Andrew 15
Giroux, Henry 16, 17, 18
Godin, Seth 15
gold open access 72–5, 77, 86
Goldberg, David Theo 8
Google 100
Google Scholar 110–11, 112, 118
Gowers, Tim 67
green open access 72, 75–7, 87
Gregory, Karen 102
Grimm, Stefan 117
Guardian, The 25–7, 133
guide at the side 5, 43, 101

H

Hamilton, Ann 132
Harris-Perry, Melissa 29, 30, 37
Harvard University 66
Havalais, Alex 55
HBO 27
higher education 19
commercialization 8–9, 47–8,
137–8
community engagement 22–3,
48–51, 53–6, 123–4, 136–7
context 14–18
democratization 8–9, 55–6, 137–8
digital media skills training 89–107,
133–4
forward thinking 54–6
inequality 40–1, 135
#InQ13 48–54
measuring scholarly impact 109–30
MOOCs 5, 39–56, 135
Open Access Network 77–8

open educational resources 81
openness 41–3
productivity 44–8
resistance to change 35–7
UK 15, 113, 115, 116–17, 134
university presses 70–1
US 14–15, 16, 78, 128
see also academics; learning;
    libraries; teaching
HIV/AIDS 59–60
Ho, Andrew 55–6
Holmwood, John 115
House I Live In, The 32
Howard, Doug 125
Hunter College, CUNY 49
hybrid publishing models 72, 73–4

I

Illuminator, The 23
Imagining New York City after stop-and-
    frisk 34
impact 2, 5–6, 15, 109–11
digital media and the rise of
    altmetrics 119–21
and engagement 121–5
forward thinking 126–30
future 134–5
Garfield 111–15
Garfield's tools and the impact
    agenda 115–19
JustPublics@365 125–6
see also metrics
inequality 18, 35, 79
in higher education 40–1, 135
#InQ13 48–54
information literacy 104–5
information overload 10–11
information retrieval 10
#InQ13 48–54, 55, 103, 136–7
open access course materials 82–4,
    85
Institute for Scientific Information
    (ISI) 112, 117
International Standard Classification
    of Education 78
Internet 1, 12, 17
impact 119
Web 2.0 22
see also blogs; massive open online
    courses; open access; social media
Invisibilia 98

iPads 10
It's complicated (boyd) 78–9

J

Jacoby, Russell 90
Jarecki, Eugene 32
Jiménez, A. C. 64, 70, 79, 85
Johnson, Allan 10–11
Jones, Sabrina 32
journal impact factor (JIF) 113–14,
    117, 119, 122
journalism 24–5, 29–37, 133
MediaCamp 94–100, 105
op-ed writing 97
Reading the Riots 25–7, 29
journals 3, 10
academic authors 61
citation analysis 112–14, 117, 119,
    122, 124
crisis 64–7, 85
gold open access 72–5, 86
green open access 75–7
hybrid publishing models 72, 73–4
journal impact factor 113–14
and MOOCs 52
open access 8, 60, 68–9, 72–7, 86
Juhasz, Alexandra 31, 55
Junnarkar, Sandeep 99, 100
Jurgenson, Nathan 10
JustPublics@365 18–19, 29–37, 133,
    138–9
#InQ13 48–54, 55, 82–4, 85, 103,
    136–7
MediaCamp 94–105, 106–7, 126,
    133
metrics 125–6, 134
open access 81–4, 85
Juxtaposition Arts 123–4

K

Karaganis, J. 122–3
Kaufman, Fred 95–6
Kelly, Blair L. M. 89
Kendrick, C. 52
Kendzior, Sarah 62, 63, 85
Kennison, Rebecca 77–8
Kimmons, R. 118
King, Jamilah 34
King, Samantha 28–9
Kirby, Paul 116–17
Klein, Ezra 97

Knoblauch, Heidi 35, 98
knowledge streams 34–5, 37
Kristof, Nicholas 89–90, 92, 105

L

Lareau, Annette 106–7
learning 5, 8, 138
  MOOCs 40–1
  participatory 42, 43
Lepore, Jill 90
libraries
  access 7, 60, 62–3, 76, 136
  card catalogs 132–3
  journals 64–7, 85
Licklider, J. C. R. 12
Lincoln, President 128
Lingua 69, 85, 137
London School of Economics (LSE)
  25–7
Louisiana State University 65
Luttrell, Wendy 36, 82

M

Martin, Glenn E. 32
Martin, Trayvon 127
massive open online courses *see*
  MOOCs
Mauer, Marc 32
Mayorga, Edwin 50
McClure, D. 122–3
McFadden, Syreeta 90, 107
media *see* journalism; social media
media literacy 104–5
MediaCamp 94–5, 105, 126
  and American Sociological
    Association 106–7
  analytics and metrics 100
  blogging 99–100
  on camera workshop 95–6
  evaluation 100–4
  information literacy 104–5
  op-ed pitches and pieces 97
  podcasting 97–8
  Twitter 98–9
metrics 5–6, 100, 107, 116–17, 139
  altmetrics 119–21, 134
  citation analysis 112–13
  journal impact factor 113–14
  JustPublics@365 125–6
  Open Syllabus Project 122–3
  and social justice 128, 129

social justice 134–5, 139
  transactional and transformational
    124–5
Mexico 73
Miller, Kristine 123–4
Mills, C. Wright 10, 24
MIT 41
Modern Language Association
  (MLA) 12
monographs 70–1
MOOCs 5, 15, 39, 41, 54–5, 135,
  136
  enclosure and commercialization
    43
  openness 41, 43, 52
  placelessness 49
  and productivity 44–8
  Udacity's failed experiment 40–1
  see also participatory, open, online
    course
Moon Illustrated Weekly 21
Morales, ed 83–4
Morris Justice Project 22–3
Murrow, Edward R. 24

N

NAACP (National Association for
  the Advancement of Colored
  People) 21
National Institutes of Health (NIH)
  27, 60, 74
National Library of Medicine 60
neighborhoods *see* communities
Nelson, Alondra 32
Nelson, Ben 46
neoliberalism 9, 16–18, 20n, 128–9,
  134
new managerialism 9, 115
New Mexico State University 66
New York City
  drug policy 32
  East Harlem 48–54, 82–3, 102–3
  Morris Justice Project 22–3
  stop-and-frisk 34
New York Times, The 32, 97
New York University Press 3, 83
New Yorker, The 24
Newburn, Tim 25–7, 133
Norberg, Lisa 77–8
note-taking 10

O

#Occupy Data 31
Occupy Wall Street 23
on camera workshops 95–6
op-ed writing 91–2, 97, 100
OpEdProject 91–2
open access 8, 60–1, 66–7, 71–2,
137
  #InQ13 82–4, 85, 136–7
  ACT UP 59–60
  books, monographs and textbooks
  78–9
  community members as copyright
  owners 83–4
  course materials for community
  engagement 82–3
  eBooks 81–2
  forward thinking 85–6
  higher education 41–3
  MOOCs 43, 48–54
  perpetually open for non-paying
  readers 72–5, 77, 86
  POOC 48–54, 55, 81, 82, 136
  pre-print, do it yourself, self-
  archiving 75–7, 87
  scholarly societies and associations
  68–9
Open Access Network (OAN) 77–8
open data 22
open educational resources (OERs)
81
Open Syllabus Project 122–3
OpenCourseWare (OCW) 41
O'Reilly, Tim 22

P

participatory, open, online course
(POOC) 48–54, 55, 81, 82–4,
85, 136
participatory research methods 22–3
Paul, Louis 25, 26, 133
peer review 2, 3, 4, 8, 61, 69
Penn State College 46, 56–7n
Pink Ribbons, Inc. 28–9
Piven, Frances Fox 22, 35
podcasts 35, 36–7, 97–8
  JustPublics@365 32–3, 34–5
police reform 22–3
Porter, Dawn 27, 28
pre-prints 75, 77
Price, Richard 72

Priem, Jason 119
productivity 44–8
professional organizations 67–70,
106–7
Public Library of Science (PLOS)
60, 73
Public Science Project 22–3
publishing *see* scholarly publishing
PubMed 60, 74

R

Race to Incarcerate (Jones) 32
racism 127–8
read-write web 22
Readalyc 73
readers 62–3
  see also open access
reading 10–11
Reading the Riots 25–7, 29, 133
Reagan, Ronald 59
'Reassessing Inequality and Re-
  Imagining the 21st-Century: East
  Harlem Focus' 48–54
*Reimagining scholarly communication for
  the 21st century* 31
Remix 123–4
Research Excellence Framework
  (REF) 15, 113, 115, 134
research impact *see* impact
*Resisting criminalization through
  academic-media-activist partnerships*
  31–2
Robert Wood Johnson Foundation
27
Roose, Kevin 97
Ruby on Rails 92

S

Sabaratnam, Meera 116–17
Sage 63, 68
sage on the stage 5, 42–3
San Francisco Declaration on
  Research Assessment (DORA)
114
San Jose State University 39–41
Sandusky, Jerry 46, 56–7n
Sayegh, Gabriel 32
scholar-activism 4, 6, 9, 21, 37, 133
  convergence and collaboration
  24–9
  in the digital era 22–3

forward thinking 37, 138
JustPublics@365 18–19, 29–37
scholarly impact *see* impact
scholarly publishing 2–4
  authors 61–2, 90
  books and monographs 70–1, 78–9
  continuous 81, 85
  copyright 51–3, 57n, 62, 80, 84,
    138
  dissertations 7
  eBooks 81–2
  future 132, 137
  gold open access 72–5, 86
  green open access 72, 75–7, 87
  hybrid models 72, 73–4
  and #InQ13 83–4
  legacy model 7–8, 61–71, 80, 85,
    92
  and MOOCs 43
  open access 8, 52–3, 60–1, 72–9,
    86, 87
  Open Access Network 77–8
  profits 63–4
  readers 62–3
  serials crisis 64–7
  and social justice 79–84
  societies and associations 67–70
  textbooks 71–2, 78–9
scholarly societies and associations
  67–70, 106–7
scholars *see* academics
scholarship
  future 131–9
  legacy model 7–8, 10, 17, 131
  transformation 2–6
  see also digital scholarship; impact;
    scholar-activism
scholarship of engagement 109–10,
  120, 121, 126–7, 129, 134
Schuman, Rebecca 12–13
SciELO 73
Science Citation Index (SCI) 112, 113,
  122
scientometrics 112, 116
Scribner, Charles 70
Segura, Liliana 32
self-archiving 75–7, 82, 84, 87
serials *see* journals
SHERPA/RoMEO 77, 84, 87
Siemens, George 41, 54, 136
Sinyangwe, Samuel 134

small private online courses (SPOCs)
  55, 136
SMOCs (synchronous massive online
  courses) 55, 136
social justice
  JustPublics@365 18–19, 30–7
  and metrics 128, 134–5, 139
  and scholarly publishing 79–84
social media 4, 89, 93
  continuous publishing 81
  measuring impact 5–6, 120, 124,
    125–6
  toolkit 33
  see also Facebook; Twitter
Social Sciences Citation Index (SSCI)
  112, 122
Sociological Images 92–3, 99, 106
SPARC (Scholarly Publishing and
  Academic Resources Coalition)
  66–7
Springer 63, 64, 68, 73, 74
Stanford University 39
Stead, Deborah 97
Stewart, Bonnie 109–10, 121
stop-and-frisk 34
Stoudt, Brett 22–3
Straus, Joseph 35
summits 31–3, 34, 35–7
synchronous massive online courses
  (SMOCs) 55, 136

T

Taylor & Francis 63, 68, 73
teaching 2, 5, 8, 42–3, 46–7
teaching quality 115
teaching score 122–3
Terras, Melissa 120
Tessler, Anne-Marie 69
textbooks 71, 85
  and MOOCs 52
  open educational resources 81
Theorizing the web 31
Thomson Reuters 117–18
Thrun, Sebastian 39, 40, 41
Torre, María Elena 22–3
training 91–4, 133–4
  forward thinking 105–7
  MediaCamp 94–105
transactional metrics 124
transformational metrics 124–5
Trubek, Anne 91–2
Tufekci, Zeynep 98

Twitter 6, 36, 93
  and academic conferences 13
  analytics 100
  curating reading 11
  information literacy 104
  scholarship of engagement 110
  workshop 98–9, 100

U

Udacity 39–41, 43
  Georgia Tech University 46, 56n
UK 115, 116–17
  Research Excellence Framework
    15, 113, 115, 134
Uniting Detroiters 22, 23
universities *see* higher education
University of California at San
    Francisco 66
University of California Press 83
University of Minnesota 123
University of Minnesota Press 83
University of Missouri 127–9, 134,
    139
University of Washington 66
US
  higher education 14–15, 16, 78,
    128
  measuring scholarly impact 116

V

Veletsianos, G. 118
Voeten, Erik 89
VozMob 4

W

Wade, Lisa 92–3, 99, 106
Washington Week in Review 30
Watters, Audrey 15, 41
Web 2.0 22
Wellcome Trust 74
Weller, Martin 2
Wells-Barnett, Ida B. 134
Westerling, Kalle 42
Whose barrio? 83–4
Wilder, Craig 128
Wiley 63, 64, 68, 73
Wilson, Darren 24
Wilson, Jennifer 129
Wolfe, Tim 127–9
women, on television 96
WordPress 99–100

Y

Yale University Press 79
YouTube 31